THE ENTREPRENEURIAL CLINICIAN

Changing healthcare from the inside out

Jo Muirhead

jomuirhead.com
purpleco.com.au

ISBN: 978-1-925846-67-6 (paperback edition)

Published by Vivid Publishing (with PurpleCo)
A division of Fontaine Publishing Group
P.O. Box 948, Fremantle
Western Australia 6959
www.vividpublishing.com.au

 A catalogue record for this
book is available from the
National Library of Australia

Book coaching and editing by Kelly Irving **kellyirving.com**
Cover design by Ellie Schroeder **ellieschroeder.com**

Note from the author
All the stories and anecdotes told in this book are based on real people,
mostly clients of mine. However, names and other details have been
changed to protect privacy. The interview transcriptions at the end of
each chapter have been reproduced with the kind permission of the
interviewees.

THE
ENTREPRENEURIAL
CLINICIAN

PRAISE FOR
THE ENTREPRENEURIAL CLINICIAN

This book is a must-read for any health professional starting a private practice or struggling to build one. In nearly 20 years of helping professionals make the shift in mindset from clinician to a clinician-entrepreneur, I've seen the same mistakes made over and over, leading to exhaustion and disillusionment. Jo shows health professionals how to embrace entrepreneurship while providing high-quality services, making a decent income, and having a healthy and balanced life. Well done, Jo!

Juliet Austin, M.A.
Marketing consultant and copywriter

Part practical advice, part inspiration and part kick in the butt, *The Entrepreneurial Clinician* provides the foundation we all need to run a successful private practice. The stories and insight apply to both experienced entrepreneurs and those starting out.

Maelisa Hall, PsyD
ENFP, psychologist, podcaster, creator

This book is a fantastic reminder to clinicians to practise what we preach! As a collective of giving people interested in helping our clients and patients to live their best life, it can be easy to forget about living our own. *The Entrepreneurial Clinician* will show you how to put your best foot forward in business, health and life and focus on the things that really matter.

Angela Lockwood
Occupational therapist, author, speaker

As an allied health professional, I can say that the word 'entrepreneurial' is not one you would naturally associate with clinicians. Somewhere in our training we are taught a mindset that counters the qualities an entrepreneur needs. But Jo shows us not only why clinicians need to think entrepreneurially, but also gives us a blueprint on how to do it. Having lived and breathed this approach herself, she makes what may seem daunting become entirely possible. Along the way, she interviews other impressive experts in the field. This is a must read for any clinician who seeks the autonomy, purpose and ownership of their own entrepreneurial journey. And let's face it – for the sake of allied health's future – we need more people armed with the necessary resources to take this journey.

Weh Yeoh
Founder OIC Cambodia and Umbo

Jo has provided an elegant structure that reconnects healthcare practitioners with their purpose. *The Entrepreneurial Clinician* provides you with an original and doable blueprint for being your best and bringing your best each and every day. So you can fall back in love with the work you do and who you do it for. If you have lost sight of why you became a healthcare practitioner then this book will reignite your passion and re-set your course.

Claire Edwards
Founder The Business of Health and b.school

I have always been impressed with Jo's coaching style and knowledge in developing the entrepreneurial clinician. Her new book is to me a guide – the beacon that points the entrepreneurial clinician to deeper, more self-reflective journey towards maintaining a successful business. In this book Jo thoughtfully drives the idea that all clinicians who venture into the world of entrepreneurship, to know their worth, exercise professional boundaries, and move into their professional brand message. As a therapist who owns several businesses, I understand what it takes to be the entrepreneurial clinician, and with this book, I believe Jo has nailed it.

Ernesto Segismundo Jr. M.S. LMFT
Adjunct Professor – Hope International University

As I read and re-read the pages of *The Entrepreneurial Clinician* I could see the many facets of my own work that has become Craig's Table. The need to reach out learn more and to dig deep inside ourselves to fill the gaps and (sometimes) chasms we see each day, to serve our clients whilst at the same time remaining on course to serve ourselves not for the faint of heart or weak of knee.

The Entrepreneurial Clinician will have you zeroing in on why and what and when (the how always tags along) this journey you are on keeps you going. My suggestion to each of you – learn, read and reread *The Entrepreneurial Clinician* often. Lean on the wisdoms that each page has to offer. Plant the seeds of the morrow knowing that you can return to *The Entrepreneurial Clinician* as oft as is needed.

It matters not which section of the allied health industry or not for profit you are from, *The Entrepreneurial Clinician* holds insights for each of you.

Rosemary McKenzie-Ferguson
Social worker, founder Craig's Table, Bags of Love and Work Injured Resource Connection

I connected with so much that was written in this book. I wish I had read it when I first started out in private practice as a medical doctor.

Being an entrepreneur is the most creative and satisfying way to thrive as a clinician. It is a mindset that can be taught. You just need to give yourself the permission to 'own it!'. Jo shows you how.

My favourite chapter was number four. We should ask ourselves, 'is this patient the right fit for me ?' 'Will they bring out the best clinician in me?'

It's okay to say NO to people! When you do this, you will say YES more often :)

This is one book I recommend all health care professionals read!

Dr Natasha Andreadis
Fertility specialist, gynaecologist, reproductive endocrinologist, clinical lecturer – University of Sydney

ABOUT THE AUTHOR

Jo Muirhead is passionate about helping people.

As an engaging speaker, coach and mentor, she empowers health professionals to take control of their own lives and build successful, sustainable and profitable practices. After all, how can you look after someone else if you're not taking care of yourself first?

A rehabilitation counsellor with over 20 years' experience, she is also the founder of PurpleCo (the Purpose for People Company), where she helps people reclaim their lives and return to work following injury, illness and trauma.

Jo started PurpleCo after becoming fed up with poor service provision for some of the most forgotten people in our communities. She has remained faithful to her vision to ensure that people come before paper and is a sought-after mentor, coach, speaker and trainer both in Australian and overseas.

As someone who lives and breathes what she teaches others, Jo has undergone a lot of trial and error to create a career and business that now works *for* her, not *against* her.

It's this knowledge and experience that she shares with others through writing and speaking for organisations, publications and podcasts like Psych Central, Thrive Global, *Huffington Post*, *Gloss*, The Private Practice Start-Up, Australian College of Applied Psychology, The Practice

Made Perfect Podcast, and many more.

Jo holds a Bachelor of Health Science majoring in Rehabilitation Counselling from the University of Sydney. She is also an accredited career counsellor though the Career Development Association of Australia, and has trained as an adult educator and coach. She was named Rehabilitation Counsellor of the Year at the 2018 Australian Allied Health Awards.

Most of her learning about private practice, however, has come from sheer determination, and a willingness to have a go and make mistakes along the way.

To Jo, a successful practice is about doing more of the work you love, with the people you want to work with, in the way you want to work. This is how you leverage your expertise, your time and your energy into a thriving business and lifestyle that contributes to a healthy system, community and world.

This is what this book will help you do.

jomuirhead.com
purpleco.com.au

ACKNOWLEDGEMENTS

When I decided to write a book, I had absolutely no idea how deep this process would make me dig within myself. I had to deal with fears and niggling voices on a daily basis that questioned, 'Am I good enough? or, 'Do I have something meaningful to say?' So there is no way I could have written this without the right people around me to support and encourage me that these were just self-doubts and that I should just keep going.

Thank you to everyone who cheered this project on and over the line. For the Facebook messages, the social media shares, the emails, the chats, and the assurance that you were waiting for this to be finished because you wanted to read it.

To my family. My husband John, thank you for believing in me and acting with grace when it was so truly needed. To my son Anthony for affirmation that the work I do is important. Thank you.

To the Latu family: Adele, Sioloa, Samuelu, Barnabas, Magdalene and Gloria, your encouragement and support of this project and of me has been a consistent breath of fresh air.

To Kelly Irving, editor and champion of doing all things well. Thank you for your tirelessness and for the times when you appeared more committed to this project than I was. Thanks to you I have a book that am proud of, that can add to the ever-growing body of knowledge that is healthcare.

To the little Irving who we haven't met yet, thank you for helping me meet the deadline!

To Nicola, thank you for 'getting me', for making sure I was OK, and for holding the space of compassion when I needed it and wasn't compassionate with myself. Your unwavering support of me as a person is greatly appreciated and much admired. Thank you.

To those who have mentored me over the past 20 years, especially to those of you who knew me right at the beginning of my own entrepreneurial journey, I thank you for your guidance, and hope you are proud of who I have become.

To Anastasia, Angela, Cathy, Dean, Jeff, Julie and Mari – thank you for being so willing to be a part of this project and for doing something rather unusual in this industry, that is, gifting your time without asking for anything in return.

To Jenny Brockis, I am so incredibly grateful that you are in my life. Thank you for believing in the work that I do and for championing the change we health professionals desire to bring about. Thank you for your courage to share your story so that we can change the way we practise. I appreciate you.

To my clinician clients, both past and present and future, this book is inspired BY YOU and is FOR YOU. It's time for us clinicians to stand up and be accountable for the change we want to see in healthcare. We can do this! Let's use this book as a resource to help us do better, to be more and to help people take back their lives – that means the people we help, as well as helping ourselves.

To clients of health services everywhere. We, the clinicians are getting it! We are understanding that to serve you to the best of our ability you actually want and need us to be performing at our best. So, for you, clients who need and want quality health care, it is my intention that we can serve you better by making sure we are looked after well.

CONTENTS

FOREWORD
BY DR JENNY BROCKIS

My goal when I first entered medical school was to follow a 'useful and practical' career path in general practice. (You know the drill.)

Now, looking back on four decades of working as a health professional, I wish I had access to Jo's book and thoughts from the very beginning. It would have saved me a lot of heartache and health problems.

One of my (then) proudest moments in my career was standing on the site of my new group medical practice in the northern suburbs of Perth. After years of sweating through exams, working horrible shifts and very long hours in the hospital system, this was my dream come true – to be my own boss, to deliver great healthcare on my terms, to create a valuable community health hub for others!

Little did I know that this building would soon become my second home (purely by counting up the hours I actually spent there), and then, eventually, my downfall.

While medical school had taught me how to conduct myself as a clinician, I had learned nothing about how to run my own business.

My business skills were painfully and laboriously accumulated by trial and error over a period of time as my practice grew.

My car journey to work started off a joy as I followed the coast north, watching surfers bobbing up and down on the sparkling water. Then it gradually became a cycle of inner dialogue. I forgot to enjoy the journey and instead kept fretting about the destination, I mean, 'How many more times over how many more years will I have to drive this route?'

My patience with my patients wore thin. I lost my curiosity as to how I could be the best of service to them, how I could best help their needs. I started asking, 'How much longer do I have to be here before I can go home?'

Worse yet, my level of fatigue was so great that every bone and every muscle ached, yet sleep (when I managed it) did nothing to restore my energy. Even my patients started to notice my dramatic weight loss. I could hear the whispers around reception, 'Is Dr Jenny alright? Does she have cancer?'

Now, my story of burnout is nothing extraordinary in the health profession – which is a complete problem in itself!

I consider myself fortunate because I made a complete recovery by taking a 'gap year' as I called it, seeking psychological help and reconnecting with this place called the big wide world and my family. I was also able to reinvent myself, or rather, rediscover the real Jenny.
But losing my practice still felt like losing a child. And when I look back, all the warning signs had long been apparent to everyone except myself.

This is what happens when we're so caught up on the hamster wheel. When we continuously give to everyone except ourselves. In the end, everyone loses out.

What I love most about the book you are about to read is that it provides you with a framework that everyone who works as a health professional needs to follow and address.

It forces you to ask the hard questions, long before you get hard-hitting answers in the form of mental illness or fatigue:

- Who am I? What do I love?

- What do I want to achieve from my work and with who?

- What do I need to do to deliver that consistently and with joy?

Nurturing self-acceptance and self-compassion through better self-care allows you the freedom to be yourself, throw off the shackles of conformity and start doing the work you know you were put on this planet to do.

As Parker Palmer author of *Let Your Life Speak* said: 'Self-care is never a selfish act – it is simply good stewardship of the only gift I have, the gift I was put on earth to offer others.' Jo's thought leadership is the antidote that we desperately need to prevent good clinicians bailing out of the health system because it is making them sick.

Her book deserves to be read by every student, every clinician and every allied health professional because as a society we cannot afford this terrible waste of human potential.

Having this book in your hands is your first great step to achieving a life you love, doing work you love to do with people you love to help.

Don't wait because otherwise it will be too late.

Dr Jenny Brockis
Speaker, author, coach, facilitator
Specialist in brain health and workplaces
that thrive
www.drjennybrockis.com

THE ENTREPRENEURIAL CLINICIAN MANIFESTO

My clients deserve the best from me,

I deserve the best from me,

Therefore, I will keep myself healthy, strong and vital.

I will practise compassion with myself,

I will practise excellence with myself,

I will practise integrity with myself,

I will keep the promises I make to myself,

I will respect my clients by charging my worth
and delivering exceptional value,

I will respect myself by acknowledging the value
I bring to others,

I will practise self-care daily,

I will BE before I DO.

I acknowledge that my work is a part of me – not all of me,

In being ME, I will be the change I want to see
in the world.

INTRODUCTION

It was a sunny Saturday and my son was quietly playing with his Lego in the lounge room. I had woken up with a horrendous migraine, once again – something that was becoming an incredibly predictable pattern. I would work hard all week, putting in long hours managing a national multi-disciplinary practice, but then when it came to the weekend, a time I was supposed to enjoy playing with my son, I had nothing left to give. I was spent, totally exhausted and very sick.

Was this the lifestyle of a competent health professional?

On the outside I looked like I had everything: I had a well-paid job with a lot of perks, I was well respected, I had family around me and I was fit. I was doing a group boot camp at 5am, three mornings a week; I was the fittest I had ever been in my life! So, being sick just didn't make any sense.

Somewhere in the migraine-induced fog, I had an a-ha moment. Here I am, the health professional who cannot get her own wellness under control. Was this all there was? To give everything I had to all of my clients, my team members and my directors and yet have nothing left for me?

This is what we as health professionals do – we give and give and give to others because we are called to help, heal and restore. Yet what about needing help, healing and restoration of our own?

To put it bluntly: I had burned out. I had reached the point that so many of us fear. And I had been living this cycle for such a long time that I actually didn't know anything different.

I came from a family where 'work' meant being useful and accepted. My parents worked hard and they taught their children that this was important in life. What they didn't teach us was the difference between hard work and *smart work*. (I'm sure you can relate.)

Instead, what I learned was that hard work comes before everything else, including your health, wellness, relaxation and enjoyment. Putting others' needs first was key.

The result? I made sure my clients were cared for, which meant I over delivered. Then they expected this over delivery as my standard. So I had to keep showing up, doing more, being more, delivering more, MORE, MORE.

Sound familiar?

We have an alarmingly high churn-and-burn rate in the healthcare sector. Smart, savvy, caring clinicians are leaving their professions in pursuit of lifestyle balance, where they can breathe, do good work, and experience a quality of life.

Health clinicians are leaving the sector in pursuit of a healthy lifestyle. Can you see the irony here?

Healthcare or health crisis?

The first step is usually to leave paid employment to start our own practice, thinking this is the golden ticket to freedom.

When we leave to set up on our own, we actually take the same problems we have working in health for an employer and create something similar in our own practice.

I speak to health professionals every week – either employed or working in their own practice – who are well on the way to burnout, mental illness or chronic disease.

How do I manage all of my business compliance and administration? How do I earn enough to keep food on the table and pay rent this month? How do I keep all my CPD (or CEUs for those of you from the USA) up to date? How do I care for myself in the midst of all of this?

The pressure of performance is still there. We are still tired. Tired of all the needs, of the ridiculous decisions that don't contribute to patient care, of more paper work to complete, of the system that we can't keep up with, of working so hard, of just *doing* all the time.

I know this because that's exactly what I experienced when I started my own practice. I thought it would 'save me'. I thought it would help set me up to use my clinical skills in a way that contributed to my health and my wellness.

But I was wrong.

You simply cannot be in the business of caring for people, until you care for yourself first.

Time to change

You entered your profession to help others and you don't want to give up that ideal, but right now, your current circumstances don't allow you to do the work you love, the way you love to do it, with the people you are best able to serve.

So this is what this book will help you do.

This book is a culmination of others' and my own life's work, successes and — more importantly — mistakes so that you don't make the same.

These days, I have a thriving private practice called PurpleCo, a practice of consultant allied health professionals who help people to return to work following injury, illness, and trauma. Plus, I am a trainer, a speaker, and a consultant to clinicians in private practice who want to build successful and sustainable businesses that work for them not against them.

The one thing my businesses have in common is that I love people. My gift is to help people, like you, bring together all the parts of a jigsaw that might be scattered in your life and help you create a whole picture again. Once that picture is formed, then you can become strong from the inside out.

We as clinicians have a lot to offer, and a lot to gain. Our clients and our patients also have a lot to gain, and a lot to offer us. To take advantage of this, we need to make some subtle shifts our thinking and our practice.

So I want you to imagine what it will be like to have the private practice of your dreams doing the work you love the way you love to do it, working with the people you are best able to serve.

Imagine going to work each day and feeling like it is effortless.

Imagine being rested, present and fully alive for your clients.

Imagine all your paperwork done, insurance claims submitted and clinical notes up to date.

Imagine having dates in your calendar to attend interesting conferences and training.

Imagine having enough money each month to put food on the table, pay the rent and look after YOU.

This is what the entrepreneurial clinician has to look forward to.

How to use this book

There are a lot of other books out there that teach you how to start a private practice, how to build a team and how to manage your money. There are a lot of other resources around to help you work on your money mindset, develop a marketing strategy and build an information product. However, what I have noticed is that there is way too much energy spent on these tactics BEFORE we have the foundations in place of WHY we are doing what we are doing.

So in Part 1 you will learn:

- why the way we operate today is working against us, not for us

- why you need to flip your thinking from clinical thinking to entrepreneurial thinking

- how to transform from feeling disillusioned to being fulfilled in your work.

In Part 2 we will explore how you become an entrepreneurial clinician through three key areas:

- who you are

- who you serve

- how you communicate.

But don't just take my word for it. So much of our work is based on fact and research from our peers, so I have also done the same in this book. Within you will read case studies and interviews with clinicians, who just like you, started somewhere, but decided they didn't like 'the system' and so implemented changes that have led them to their success.

On the way, you will also find exercises to help you on your own journey to becoming an entrepreneurial clinician. You may like to use the notes section of this book to help you complete them, otherwise you can also download separate worksheets from my website: **www.jomuirhead.com. au/book**.

It is my intention in writing this book that your gift to the work, your practice, will be reinvigorated. That you will leave the pages of this book knowing without any doubt that you are not just needed in this day and age, YOU ARE NECESSARY!

That means ALL of you: healthy mind, body and business.

Jo

The entrepreneurial clinician

- Are you in, or aspiring to be in, a private practice of your own, building a caseload of clients you love while creating a lifestyle that meets your financial, family, wealth creation, self-care needs?

- Do you fantasise about being able to do your clinical work in a way that you know will bring results for your clients, if only you could be left to do the work?

- Do you want to see real long-lasting change, without all the frustration that comes from obstacles preventing the change?

- Do you want to build a group practice, or a multi person practice, where you grow, nurture and develop a team of other entrepreneurial clinicians?

- Do you long for a framework to be able to integrate your care of self and the care of your clients with financial gain and lifestyle benefits, all while remaining passionate and engaged by your work?

- Would you like to see clients therapeutically, but also through paid speaking opportunities, or by providing training or workshops?

- Do you want to have a bigger influence than simply seeing one client at a time?

- Would you like to monetise your knowledge and skills, using affiliates, or product partnerships, or building a range of online delivery products?

- Are you employed by someone else right now, but have a side hustle, with the opportunity to create and grow new service delivery streams or alternative sources of income?

- Would you like to move around these types of enterprise and income streams based on your desire, needs and wants in the moment?

- Do you want to work with the people you want to work with, in the way you want to work?

This is what awaits you as an entrepreneurial clinician.

INTERVIEW
ANGELA LOCKWOOD
OCCUPATIONAL THERAPIST, AUTHOR,
SPEAKER, CHAMPION OF PEOPLE

Angela has dedicated her life to being a pediatric occupational therapist (OT), advising families on how to bring the energy and focus they need to all they do, despite what challenges are thrown at them. She is equally at ease working with children as she is standing in front of a packed audience delivering a keynote.

Today Angela lives her passion, energy, and experience through speaking, training, facilitating and writing books. She is the author of the bestselling *Switch Off: How to Find Calm in a Noisy World.*

I love and have learned so much from this book that I insist my coaching clients read it as part of working with me (so I recommend you do too!).

....

How has occupational therapy provided you with this amazing platform that so many other people dream of?

What I love about OT and not just really OT specifically, but health professionals generally, is that we really are very giving people. Usually we see the good in other people and we want to help bring that out. So really the thing that helped me become an OT was that I had a lived experience myself where I had quite a traumatic injury and I came across an OT who would come and see me in hospital. After the visit, I would think, 'That person is a remarkable human being, that's what I want to be.'

I have a natural tendency as a human to go, 'yeah, there's a problem, but surely there's a way that we can either work with this or look at things differently.' That's what I love about OT. OTs do that just naturally. We become solution finders rather than looking at the negatives.

So how has that helped you transition from working in your practice to writing and speaking at corporate events?

OTs look at a person in their entirety, and also in the environment that they operate it in, so it could be in a workplace, it could be in a family, it could be as a child in a school. We look at a whole person and we realise that the body and the mind are really connected. So, I've got the body, the mind, the spirit, all of those things to consider. If something is out of whack, if something is out of alignment, then everything else becomes out of alignment.

I really believe that OT has provided me with skills to be able to look at any issue, whether it be in a corporate environment or something else, and take a step back from it all, and go, 'Okay, I can see what's going on here, now where can my skill set most be effective?' I don't jump straight into the problem, I say, 'What are the issues and how do we solve them?'

I think for health professionals we have a unique way of

looking at things. We have a really unique heart-centred approach, but it's very systematic and very problem solving. So that's where my fundamental learnings of OT have really helped me in whatever environment I've found myself in, whether it be working one-on-one as a mentor with executives, or speaking to people about how they can switch off or how they can make better decisions.

It's really going, 'What value can I offer this situation and how can I bring out the best in the situation that I'm working in?'

What do you think an entrepreneurial clinician is?

I absolutely love that you even asked this question because I think entrepreneurial clinician is really where we're moving forward, where we're moving as an industry. But I think entrepreneurism is so over used now that people have actually forgotten what it means.

My personal interpretation (because it is really open to interpretation) is people who look for and create opportunities. So that's the definition according to me. I don't think it's in any dictionary, but if I can just say really, an entrepreneur, in essence, is somebody who can take a step back and go, 'What opportunities are there in front of me or in front of this situation and how can I maximise that, and how can I create better value?'

So I'm a CEO right now and for me to operate the best that I can as a CEO or an entrepreneur, whatever that looks like, requires me to have skills in other areas to be able to keep progressing forward and to ensure that what I'm doing is sustainable, that I can do it at the level I choose to do it and take it wherever it is that I want to take it.

We need to be really clear around what our value offering is. When we can do that, opportunities present themselves to us and we can decide whether or not we are going to be the best person for that gig or not.

That's really, I believe, what entrepreneurism really is, and where being an entrepreneurial clinician is going. These are really exciting times for clinicians and people I think should get really, really excited. Not just for the potential for themselves and the industry, but also for the people we're working with.

I think, people should look at it around maximising and growing. This presents us with so many possibilities, it's awesome.

I think in the past we would become a little bit stagnant going down just a clinician route, but entrepreneurial clinician, that's exciting science!

What opportunities do you think entrepreneurial thinking can offer health professionals?

Definitely looking outside of our industry is a really big opportunity now. We have information at our fingertips, so we can look for anything we want at the click of a button. So it's not the lack of information that's a problem, it's actually how do we translate the information that's available to us, and I watch a lot of clinicians who are becoming really savvy in this entrepreneurial space, and they're putting their own spin in a modern time on age old information.

The information has been around forever, but what they're doing is, they are going, 'How can we make this information current so that people are excited by the information?' I really believe that that's something where we can only bring ourselves into that. We can't copy off other people. You can only bring our own energy and professionalism to it.

I think that's a really big opportunity for us at the moment, to be able to translate the information into really practical ways, but also to look outside of our industry into business realms and how these other people are doing it. It's not stealing ideas, it's just trying to learn from other industries who have either messed up themselves, have made the mistakes, how can we not make the mistakes and just learn from them.

So what becomes the biggest challenges for clinicians and health professionals on this new journey?

What that's making me realise is there's quite a saturated market that's coming through, that we've never seen before. People are having to get really business savvy. In the past they really could just get by on their clinical expertise, but now what they're having to do is become quite privatised, which will mean they have to become really good at marketing and really good at understanding the psychology behind selling and tapping into those people who are outside of our industry that can help us to grow our business and even scale a business.

For years, my job was really helping health professionals to become clear in business, and what I'm noticing is those that jumped on board five or six years ago, now are just sailing, they're flying with their business. But those that didn't think that it was going to be a priority are now starting to go, 'Whoops, what have I done? I've got to play catch-up now.'

One of the biggest challenges is health professionals realising the importance of doing business well, and having a heart-led business that makes money.

I think the other big challenge is health professionals thinking we need to do it all on our own. But we don't have to do everything. We can't be the fountain of all knowledge on everything. So again, I go back to one of the things I said really at the beginning, be really clear on what your unique value offering is, as a clinician, as a human being.

What is the thing that you can bring to the world?
For everything else, there are other people who
have got amazing skill sets in that area.

Then everyone gets to work together, and dare I say it, the world will be a better place. People won't be running around, and will be providing, really, really great innovative entrepreneurial practice.

What is the one thing you would encourage any health professional to be successful in their clinical career, and would this be different to what an entrepreneurial clinician needs to be?

Always remember what your value is. I've said this quite a few times; be really clear on what your value offering is. And that doesn't just mean a monetary value, it actually goes right back to what is the thing?

There is nothing that lights me up better than working with children. I love adults of course, I love the work I do in that space, but if I was to get you in a room and really tap into my passion area, it's really making sure that kids have the best start in life, and that's the thing that gets me excited.

Second, get good at business. Don't put it in the too hard basket. People need the very best of you, and they need to really get all that great stuff from you, not the stuff that's left when you're running around like a chicken with its head cut off.

Getting good at business, you don't have to know all of it inside and out, but what you do have to do is have a good understanding of it. Then tap into those people who are great at it.

For example, I have an accountant, I don't want to know anything about accountancy, but what I do need to know, is how to read the numbers. Because without the numbers, and without that great business, I can't give the best to my clients because I've got no money to go to training, to get my professional development skills happening, to be able to tap into great people who can support me to build my business.

Allied health professionals, I think, are a little bit worse in this space. I'm making a very generalised comment, but doctors are pretty good at it. They're pretty good at being good at business. They're good at setting up systems around them to make them good at business.

Be clear on your own value and become good at business.

When those two come together, you've got a brilliant practice that you'll be doing for the next 20 years and you'll be loving it.

Part 1

WHY YOU NEED TO CHANGE

WE LIVE IN AN AGE OF INFORMATION overload, digital demand and rate and review. Clients now come to us with a lot of knowledge and even greater expectations on how we will treat them – not just as a cluster of symptoms or a diagnosis – but as a whole person.

However, our education and clinician supervision has not prepared us for this. We continue to be educated by institutions that demand we as professionals treat ALL the people with ALL of the problems, ALL the time (and for less than an average wage). We need to be switched on ALL of the time, which means we have little time or energy left to process, explore, consult or think.

We have alarming rates of churn-and-burn in our healthcare sector. We are churning out new graduates from university straight into workplaces where they are expected to perform from day three, without adequate supervision, training and mentoring. The result? They burn out so that they feel they have no choice but to leave. Then we churn through health professionals in our workplaces, throwing more demands on them (you), compliance, paperwork and increasing hours. The result? They burn out and they leave.

So where will all the experienced, passionate and savvy health professionals be? If there is no one left to treat the people who need treating, then how is anyone going to get the help they need?

The healthcare system has set us up to fail as employed clinicians and private practice owners. It is failing us because so many of us are seeking alternatives to the work we trained so long and hard to do.

Healthcare, like any institutionalised system, changes at glacial speed. We and our clients cannot afford to wait – we have to be the change for ourselves and for our clients.

This means approaching how we do our work with a new way of thinking. By changing our mindset and the way we do business we can have, not just the freedom and flexibility that we crave, but also the feeling of fulfilment that we long for.

This is what we will discover in Part 1.

Chapter one

System overload!

I WAS WORKING WITH A CLIENT, funded by an insurance company, where I remember being on the telephone to a claim assessor who was telling me how to run my case. My client was a young apprentice, who had broken his arm at work. According to the claim assessor (a high school graduate with administration knowledge and skills only), this injury should have healed within six weeks and there was no need for any more service, therefore, why was I still involved? Why was I still travelling to meet with the client and his employer?

I tried my best to calmly explain – again – that this young man had suffered a displaced fracture to the radius in his right forearm, which required surgery to pin and plate it. I also explained that the incident that caused this young man to break his arm involved dodging an angle grinder that had been thrown at him by his boss – the very same person who was managing his return to work.

But, like what usually happens, I was being told how to do my work, the very thing that I am an expert in, by someone who had little-to-no health training because 'it was not needed in this role'. This was the last straw for me. I was done. If I could not do the work the way I knew it needed to be done, then I didn't want to do this work anymore.

I have heard countless stories like this from health professionals in hospitals, community centres, larger agencies and private practices. The common theme is: *I can't to this work the way I know it needs to be done.*

It's stifling. We end up resentful, we end up disengaged, we end up burned out. And it is our clients who suffer.

> *We are frustrated because the system we work in does not allow us to do the actual work.*

What is it really costing us?

Many of us leave employment and set up our own practices with the expectation that we will find the freedom and flexibility to do the work the way we it needs to be done. But if we take the same models of delivery with us, that freedom and flexibility won't eventuate.

When I ask health professionals what they think is wrong with healthcare and what types of change they would like to see I rarely get responses about changing the model of delivery, or of client expectations of the clinician. The response I get is that governments need to make available more money to fund more clinicians to provide more services for free. We need more beds, more staff – and what about more 'talent'?

Those of us who have created healthcare businesses are faced with a revolving door of talent acquisition and recruitment costs. We onboard, train and develop team members who then leave us. In effect, this means our capacity to train and develop comprehensively, thoroughly and appropriately is decreasing. And in the meantime, the cost of business and the demands of compliance is increasing.

There continues to be a relentless tension for us between taking care of the people in need while remaining financially afloat.

At the end of the day – we need to eat too! We have children to feed, school fees to pay, and god forbid we ever think about having a holiday.

Our intentions have always been noble, our desire has always been one of care, however, when the rubber hits the road, we too need to ensure we have a roof over our heads. We need to pay back our student loans and make sure our family is looked after. We want, no we need, a work life that allows us to be well taken care of.

In the meantime, we continue to exhaust our bodies, minds and skills in an effort to keep up with these increasing demands.

The lack of control over our work is a leading cause of disengagement, and burn out amongst health professionals. This is due to the sheer numbers of people we see, the pace at which we work, and the method of work that is imposed upon us.

Worse yet, burn out leads to mistakes, which leads to harm of the people in our care.

So while yes, the government has a role to play in healthcare, we as individual clinicians have a bigger responsibility in bringing about the change that we desperately seek.

We are the change

It's all well and good to say the government and the big end of town need to change, however, they won't – or if they do it will be at glacial speed. (Surely, I don't have to convince you of that fact.)

So, if we do nothing and keep perpetuating passive models of healthcare then we really have no one else to blame but ourselves when clients argue about paying our full fee. Or when work feels like a struggle every day just to make ends meet.

If we as clinicians working in the health sector do NOTHING then we are just contributing to the problem.

We need to take ownership for ourselves and find a new way to work within this system, a way that works for us, not against us.

So I want you to imagine a healthcare system that actually creates a culture of change. Imagine a healthcare system in which our clients take responsibility and ownership for their own recovery, health and wellness, and they are resourced to do so.

Imagine a healthcare system where every one of us as clinicians is financially rewarded for the value we bring to the lives we change. Imagine a health system where we want to work because the work is fulfilling.

Now imagine what would happen if we stopped complaining about what is not working and started looking for ways to make it work for us.

A new age

My parents' generation saw the treatment provider as the expert. Almost like a god, especially in western society where the doctor, the physiotherapist, the health professional gave an opinion, provided a prescription or gave them something to do, and they just believed them. They trusted them to get it right, they trusted them to make them better.

Now our clients are our customers. They turn up to the initial meeting with incredible knowledge about their condition, their diagnosis and their treatment options. Sometimes they even come armed with a proposed 'treatment plan' based on what they have read or heard about their condition. And they are ready to rate and review us online after they have left the session.

Of course, our degrees and years of clinical experience can't be replaced with a Google search, but what this is telling us is that our clients want to be informed. They want to *partner with us* in their healthcare and recovery. They have a choice, and they can choose NOT to work with us.

We are no longer seen as god.

Our clients demand to be treated differently from way we are used to providing care. But rather than seeing this as yet another demand, we can flip our thinking to see this as an opportunity.

Our clients, the people we serve, don't just want to be a number, or a syndrome or a diagnosis, they want to know we care. Our biggest opportunity for engagement with them is our ability to show we are human, that we are passionate about the work we do and that we can think outside the box when it comes to solutions. An internet search cannot offer this experience!

Sure, we still need professionalism and ethics. However, it's our passion for people that will completely revoluntise the system in which we work, and the system in which we build a sustainable practice. This is the only way we will stop feeling trapped and start feeling alive!

This kind of systemic change means each of us must start thinking outside of the box we work in — we need to become entrepreneurs.

From clinician to entrepreneur

It wasn't that long ago, that the word 'entrepreneur' had very little relevance to me. It was a title given to people who built vast empires, made a lot of money and turned everything to gold wherever they went. Agree?

I often think of an entrepreneur as someone with a lot of vision and the drive to get a business moving and off the ground. Someone who looks for how an industry works and then disrupts it by doing the complete opposite (think about the founders of Uber and Airbnb, for example).

We consider them to be brave, passionate, community-minded and someone with a strong tolerance to risk and adversity. Which sounds completely ludicrous when you try and apply this thinking to clinicians running private practices right! We are health professionals by training, and because of the incredible importance of the work we do with people, we are by nature risk averse and process oriented. We have many checks, balances and compliances to ensure we maintain standards of patient care.

Make a mistake as an entrepreneur and you may end up changing the world for good. However, make a mistake as a clinician and people can be harmed, we could lose our job, or worse, end up with a malpractice suit.

Yet remember, the old school way of working no longer works for us. Our clients demand MORE from us, our system is failing them, as a result, we are struggling, burned out and unhappy. We cannot sit around on our hands and just wait for answers or solutions to magically appear. We have to adopt a new way of working, which means being willing to flip our thinking on how we add VALUE to the lives of others, as well as our own, as Figure 1.1 shows.

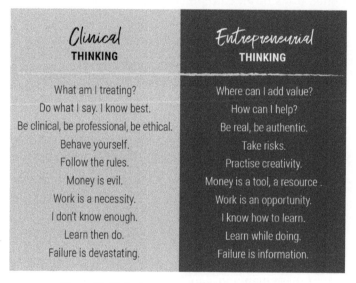

Clinical THINKING	*Entrepreneurial* THINKING
What am I treating?	Where can I add value?
Do what I say. I know best.	How can I help?
Be clinical, be professional, be ethical.	Be real, be authentic.
Behave yourself.	Take risks.
Follow the rules.	Practise creativity.
Money is evil.	Money is a tool, a resource .
Work is a necessity.	Work is an opportunity.
I don't know enough.	I know how to learn.
Learn then do.	Learn while doing.
Failure is devastating.	Failure is information.

Figure 1.1: Clinical versus entrepreneurial thinking

To be successful in any business — and that includes healthcare — there must be a level of risk taking, which means a level of being OK with making mistakes and failure.

Turn risk into gain

In mentoring health professionals over the past six years I've been struck by those who seem to have an innate ability to grab hold of the entrepreneur within them and those who don't. The transition from health professional to entrepreneur is more difficult for some than others, and the key to this is differing attitudes to risk.

As health professionals we are always following a technique. We practise a modality. When we are dealing with a tricky client or pathology we rely on the process. We go back to the evidence, we review best practice in clinical care, we practise our craft until it becomes almost innate. We know we have to be on the ball because if we aren't, the effects of poor decisions could be really disastrous for our clients.

To manage the risk of being a health professional we maintain our credentials, we participate in clinical supervision, we have mandatory PD points or hours we need to achieve in a given timeframe. In short, we continue to prove ourselves worthy of our profession.

We are motivated by the stick rather than the carrot. Our focus is, 'I can't let this client down', 'I can't let my profession down', 'I can't let myself down by making a mistake'.

Just think of how betrayed we feel when we hear of someone who gets it wrong, we all judge thinking, 'How did that happen?' 'They mustn't have been supervised well enough, or kept their credentials up to date, or maintained their professional standards.'

All healthcare (as opposed to wellness) is about mitigating risk, mitigating loss. Hence, we tend to be cautious, risk averse and conservative. We often call this ethical or professional – which it is. No argument here.

But risk averse, cautious and conservative are not the ingrained attitudes of successful entrepreneurs or business owners.

The reason why some health professionals build successful and sustainable businesses and others just get stuck in the process of trying to build a business is their different views about risk.

You must manage the inner conflict between:

- risk averse v risk taker
- caution v courage
- conservative v radical.

You need to learn to take risks and accept that not all risk taking is bad.

You need to identify what you can risk and what you cannot.

I am NOT saying it's time to stop practising clinical decision making, nor am I saying it's time to stop being professional or ethical. No in fact we need to be all these things AND more.

We need to understand that entrepreneurial thinking in western workplaces is a new literacy.

While health professionals and entrepreneurs appear to be on two different ends of the mindset spectrum, it's important you learn to become BOTH an entrepreneur and a clinician at the same time.

So how might you practise this in your work?

- When you see a client struggling with something new, bring it to their attention, offer advice, don't let them suffer when you know you can help.

- Advocate for self-learning and always ask clients how you can help.

- Always be present and focused when with your clients.

- Ask clients to take a little risk sometimes, for example, to try walking downstairs, or to be in the moment with an uncomfortable emotion, or to use their body in a way that might cause some pain.

- Rarely treat two clients exactly the same way.

- Ask clients to use their time, their energy, their resilience, their coping skills every single day.

- Understand that money is a tool, it's a resource, it allows you to invest in those things that are important to you.

- Help your clients understand that learning and practising a new skill propels them towards their goal.

- Use failure as information, for example, that exercise didn't work for that client at this time, therefore, let's find another way.

For a health professional to become a successful and happy business owner they have to bring these two conflicting paradigms together.

Seize the opportunity

Learning to think and behave like an entrepreneurial clinician requires two things:

1. **Acceptance** of the enormous opportunities that this mindset and way of thinking provides us.

2. **Acknowledgement** that with this great opportunity comes incredible personal responsibility.

Being an entrepreneurial clinician affords us with tremendous opportunities.

Opportunities to create the work–life balance that we crave. To let go of the nine to five, the four weeks annual leave a year and the 10 days sick leave. To let go of antiquated ways of doing things, to leverage time, energy, knowledge and skill. To work in a way that is fulfilling. To engage a wider audience to bring about more change to more people in your specific area of passion and expertise.

I have spoken to hundreds of clinicians in the past seven years from all over the world (some of whom are included in this book), and pretty much every one says they want the same thing:

- choice

- freedom

- flexibility

- finances to fund choice, freedom and flexibility.

This is possible! This is possible when you change your thinking and the way in which you work to become BOTH clinical and entrepreneurial.

The best thing is that when you create choice, freedom and flexibility, you start to feel fulfilled.

That's exactly what we look at doing in Chapter 2.

INTERVIEW
MARI A LEE
PSYCHOTHERAPIST, COACH,
AUTHOR, ADVOCATE, SPEAKER

Mari A Lee, LMFT, CSAT-S has been a successful businesswoman and entrepreneur for over 30 years. She is a licensed marriage and family therapist, a certified sex addiction therapist and supervisor, and the founder of Growth Counseling Services, a busy private practice in Southern California.

Mari is also a bestselling author of multiple books, a popular national speaker in the US, and a respected and trusted business coach for therapists all across the United States and internationally.

Mari and I first met in person in 2015 when we were both presenters at a conference in La Jolla, California. As I have got to know her over the years, I have been inspired by her innate gift at turning her passion into a way of life, her ability to create opportunity, and to lead change wherever she goes.

Some of the things I admire about Mari (which in all honesty intimidated me at first) are her commitment to kindness, ethics and professionalism, and supporting mental health professionals to be their best selves.

Mari is a shining example of how we as clinicians can maintain our professionalism while compassionately meeting the needs of clients, and authentically supporting colleagues to fulfill their dreams.

....

What made you decide to pursue therapy as the next step in your work–life?

Having grown up for a few years in the foster care system with very little money and no family to fall back on, I believe I was born with the entrepreneur DNA. On my own at 16 years of age, I worked many different jobs during those challenging teen years in order to support myself. Some of those early jobs included everything from working in strawberry fields picking berries, to babysitting, to cleaning houses, to selling seashell necklaces on the beach.

After juggling several of these odd jobs trying to scrape by, by the time I was 18, I realised I needed to learn a trade so that I could get ahead, save money for a car, and go to college.

I decided to attend cosmetology school during the day, and worked a fast food job at night, and did my studying in between. A year later, after a lot of hard work and very little sleep, I had my license to practice hair and makeup, something I'd always enjoyed doing.

I honed my craft over the next two years working for other salon owners. Eventually I thought, 'Wouldn't it be cool if I could start my own business providing hair cutting and styling services to busy executives?' After months of researching how to do this, asking endless questions, learning the ropes, and with many mistakes along the way, I started my first business, California Cuts.

What started off as a humble little professional dream grew beyond what I ever imagined. After a few years, I sold my business for a nice profit. I used the money to go back to school, to add to my savings account, and to purchase a car. I attended college classes in the evening while working in a law firm as a receptionist, and doing hair and make-up on the weekends.

This eventually led to an opportunity to manage a graphic design department in a well-known financial investment firm. It was a whole new world for me and I enjoyed the fast-paced corporate environment. This career also allowed me to purchase my first home at 29 years old, something that I was very proud of as a former foster care kid – a home that I still own to this day.

After several years with this firm, in my early 30s and burned out from the competitive pace, I was ready for a change. I decided once again to return to college and advance my design skills. It was around this time that I opened my second business, Eden Design and Interiors, where I provided interior design and wedding planning services.

Several years later, after successfully growing my design firm, I was once again feeling ready for a change of pace. I was contacted by an executive placement company with an offer to return to corporate America working for a fundraising organisation for rescue missions.

The clients of the missions I oversaw were veterans dealing with PTSD, mentally ill individuals, abused children, addicts in recovery, domestic violence survivors, and schizophrenics. It was an honor to support these courageous people who were desperately trying to create better lives. And it was a job that was near and dear to my heart having once been a homeless teen myself.

Though I managed multi-million dollar budgets and worked with top executives, it was during this time that I discovered my calling as a therapist. In helping the rescue missions' sweet clients I connected with what I call my 'soul work' as a psychotherapist.

Little did I know the long road that was ahead of me in deciding to attend graduate school! I remember saying to my sister (also a former foster care kid), 'I'll be 45 years old before I have my masters degree, maybe it's too late for me to do this?' My sister wisely responded, 'God willing you will turn 45 anyway, you may as well do so with a masters degree pursuing work you feel led to do. I'll help you!'

Together we managed to pay for every single class, semester after semester, year after year, out of our own pockets in order to avoid my having to have student loans at mid-life. Then came the long years of clinical internship, and then studying for, and passing the two grueling licensing exams.

The day finally came when I was a licensed psychotherapist, hooray! Overtime I built a thriving private practice, became a trusted coach to other clinicians, and a published author and national speaker.

It wasn't easy to accomplish these dreams, not by a long shot. It was tough, but also very rewarding.

Do you have a definition of what an entrepreneur is?

For me entrepreneur means to provide trusted services and products offered with skill, gratitudeand integrity. It means dedication, elbow grease, and believing in yourself – even if no one else does.

Additionally, a successful entrepreneur must have good boundaries around one's time. Equally important is to invest in on going self-care that includes regular time off. This is a skill that took me a while to learn!

However, the sacred core of what it means to be an entrepreneur for me is to honour my god-given gifts and talents, while I honor and support the gifts and talents of others.

It's about doing the things that I love to do, to work with the people that I love to work with, to make my own schedule, to have the freedom to say yes to projects that make my heart sing, and to say no to what doesn't.

To enjoy the fruits of my labour while investing in the people, places and things that I love the most in this world. To practice generosity and to pass the blessings I've been given on to others. People have their own definition of success, but this is what success feels like to me.

Entrepreneurship is also about creativity and resilience – you have to be willing to roll up your sleeves, to take responsible risks, to make room for disappointments, to own your mistakes (and we all make them!), and to operate in integrity.

A smart entrepreneur also understands that they can't and should not do it all on their own. Every wise businessperson invests in an even wiser team of supportive people. 'There is no strength where there is no struggle,' Oprah Winfrey often says, however, one does not have to struggle alone.

One of the aspects I dearly love about my career is business coaching, and my coaching clients are therapists and clinicians. I deeply enjoy helping each colleague define their vision and reach their professional goals and dreams. My motto is: when one healer succeeds, we all succeed!

What I have come to realise after 10 years of supporting healers is that while I can teach people tools, I can teach them programs and systems, I can teach them how to write a book, how to give a speech, how to sell an online course, how to market, how to organise their business, and help them with confidence building, I cannot teach somebody what I call the art and soul of being an entrepreneur.

While there are tools I teach my coaching clients to achieve their professional goals, each entrepreneur must dig deep and find what truly sets their heart on fire. One's own unique passion is not something that can be taught.

What new advances in the healthcare profession are you excited about?

1. Telemental health

I've been enjoying providing telemental health sessions to therapy clients. I love that we now have a variety of excellent HIPAA compliant platforms in the US for this type of therapy.

Telehealth sessions are especially helpful for professionals with tight schedules, or busy mums who don't have a lot of extra time, or people who are struggling with chronic illnesses or physical challenges, or elderly individuals where driving in traffic is not an option.

Telehealth is a beautiful way to reach individuals who need counseling support within one's licensure area. And it is a great alternative for counselling clients who prefer the convenience of a session from their home or office.

2. Walk and talk therapy

I started walk/talk therapy with my patients about 12 years ago. It was virtually unheard of at that time; I'm so encouraged to see other colleagues now providing this service to help clients walk and talk their way through challenges as they heal and move forward, literally and figuratively, in their lives and relationships. There is growing research on the benefits of walk/talk therapy, and it is a service that my clients have embraced and enjoy.

3. Multiple income streams

As an entrepreneur, and especially if you are a therapist, it is wise to develop multiple income streams in order to avoid burnout. Ask yourself, 'How can I support a hurting person heal beyond the one-on-one therapy hour? Is it a course that I can sell online? A webinar I can develop? An e-book I can write?'

My specialisation in my therapy practice is working with sexually addicted men and their betrayed spouse or partner. In order to create passive income, I wrote my first book, *Facing Heartbreak: Steps to Recovery for Partners of Sex Addicts,* several years ago because, as a former wounded partner of a sexually compulsive person, I wanted women and men around the world to have access to therapy exercises to help them on their healing journey.

I recently published my second eBook, *Healing Betrayal,* for the hurting spouse or partner who has just found out that their significant other has been cheating on them. Perhaps this person is searching the internet, angry and scared to death, crying their eyes out. My hope is that they find *Healing Betrayal,* and no matter where they are located in the world, they can quickly download this informative, compassionate roadmap and learn about the first healing steps they need to take.

What are some of the biggest challenges for clinicians and health professionals who want to embark on an entrepreneurial journey?

The road through graduate school, clinical internship and launching a private practice can feel daunting at times. However, keep your eye on the prize! Remember why it is that you wanted to be a therapist and/or business owner. Create affirmations, read them often, and trust that you can do this…one day at a time.

Even though most of your fellow healers will be helpful and kind, unfortunately you will occasionally run across the 'Negative Nellies', 'Fearful Freds', and 'Envious Irmas'. They exist – even in our clinical field. And when you do, be polite, be kind, have good boundaries, and don't engage in the pettiness. Move on and leave them in your rearview mirror and find a healthy professional tribe who has your back, celebrates your successes, and offers support during the challenging times.

I believe in treating people how you wish to be treated. Maya Angelou, an author I love, once wrote, 'People will forget what you say, people will forget what you do, but people will never forget how you made them feel.'

And this is so very true. Good or bad, we never forget how people made us feel.

What is something you could offer to encourage a healing professional who wants to be successful in their clinical career or health business?

To the lovely human being reading this, *please* trust your gifts.

And, as stated earlier, find a tribe of people who will be the wind under your wings, who will have your back, who will celebrate your wins, who will help you when you fall on your knees – because we all start somewhere, and we all fall down now and then.

Understand that you have a lot to offer this world. Even if somebody wrote five books on the same topic that you want to write a book on, your vision will be fresh and unique and your audience will need to read the words that *you've* written. *Your* words are important.

Clearly there is a reason that you have picked up this special book. Please trust that you are able to create a thriving business. If this former homeless foster kid can do it, you can too!

And if you struggle in a particular area of business, if you need support (and we all do now and again), find somebody who can assist you with those particular tasks, or help you learn the skills you need in growing your vision from little dream seedlings, to a blossoming abundant garden.

Finally, and this is the most important thing I can share: if you don't like the work that you do, please don't do it for five more flipping minutes.

To clarify, I understand that each of us needs to earn money to live. I pay my own mortgage and my own bills, and I've worked my entire life, so believe me I understand that you can't just up and quit your job.

But please give yourself a permission slip to start the baby steps in finding something else that you'll love doing. And trust that god, or whatever you call your higher power, is in the details and that doors will open for you.

In closing, I encourage you to trust that you have a whole set of professional gifts that the world around you is waiting for. We need *your* voice. We need *your* skills. We need *you*.

And remember:
keep it kind, keep it fresh, keep it real,
and trust that you've got this!

Chapter two

From disillusioned to fulfilled

WHEN I WAS EMPLOYED IN government and private enterprise I felt trapped. I felt trapped by the expectations of productivity and administration, I felt trapped by the way I was supposed to do things. I felt trapped by not having control over my work load, and by not having control over the work I was doing with clients. I felt trapped by my work and I longed for the weekend.

I know this is how you feel, too.

Everywhere groups of clinicians in private practice gather (online, offline, at a conference, just at lunch or over drinks), the conversation will eventually focus on why they decided to start their own private practice – more importantly, how it feels a very long way from the vision they originally had.

One of the biggest influences on my decision to go out on my own was a belief that I would be free from being told what to do by people who didn't have a clue about the work I was doing. I believed that was how I would be able to see real change in my clients' lives and that would make me feel good, happy and fulfilled.

I expected that I would have greater control over my workload because I could say YES or NO to the work I wanted to do.

I expected to make as much money as I did as a salaried employee, and I expected that there would be tax benefits for being self-employed that would contribute to my wealth creation and financial future.

I also expected to feel free because I was setting my own hours and doing the work when I wanted to do it the way I wanted to do it.

How wrong was I!

Six weeks into PurpleCo, I had more work than I knew what to do with. I had a caseload of 14 clients, generating about $2K per week. This stunned me, because I had always had caseloads as high as 40 clients, sometimes even 50 clients.

I (like you) had been living in a false sense of security.

You see I did not factor in all the admin and extras that comes along with clients that add (no – drain) your time during the week. I just focused on the fact I was attracting clients! Clients who were paying me money! And I thought I had the freedom to do what I wanted!

But then my ego got in the way.

My customers noticed that I was doing good work, so this attracted MORE customers (YAY) and more paperwork (NO!).

I got scared that if I said no to people, I would lose out on business. So I said yes, to everything. (Sound familiar?)

I found myself juggling client and customer demands. I found myself working most weekends to catch up on reports, bookkeeping, notes and emails (oh, the emails!). My hours went from 30 to 60 to 80 hours a week. I felt like I was running late on so many things that I would over commit and over function in an effort to prove that I was good enough. It's a vicious cycle, right?

This is not freedom, this is being enslaved.

Freedom is a choice, not a trap

Hands up if you went into business for yourself wanting flexibility? Yep, me too. I wanted to work closer to home, I wanted to set my own hours, I didn't want to work with absolutely everyone.

I wanted all my needs to be met, without a fear of lack or uncertainty. I thought that employment was a trap. But actually, the trap was my own sense of self in my work.

The trap was not knowing myself well enough to know how to make private practice work best for me.

I was enslaved by my fears and doubts that I had to say YES to everything otherwise the money would run out, or I would stop getting clients.

Freedom, on the other hand, is about your ability to choose in any given moment. Freedom is about knowing who you are, who you serve and how you serve them.

Freedom is actually something we choose to experience every single day.

When you do this, when you start to make more conscious choices, then you start to move from feeling disillusioned by your business to feeling fulfilled by it, as shown in Figure 2.1.

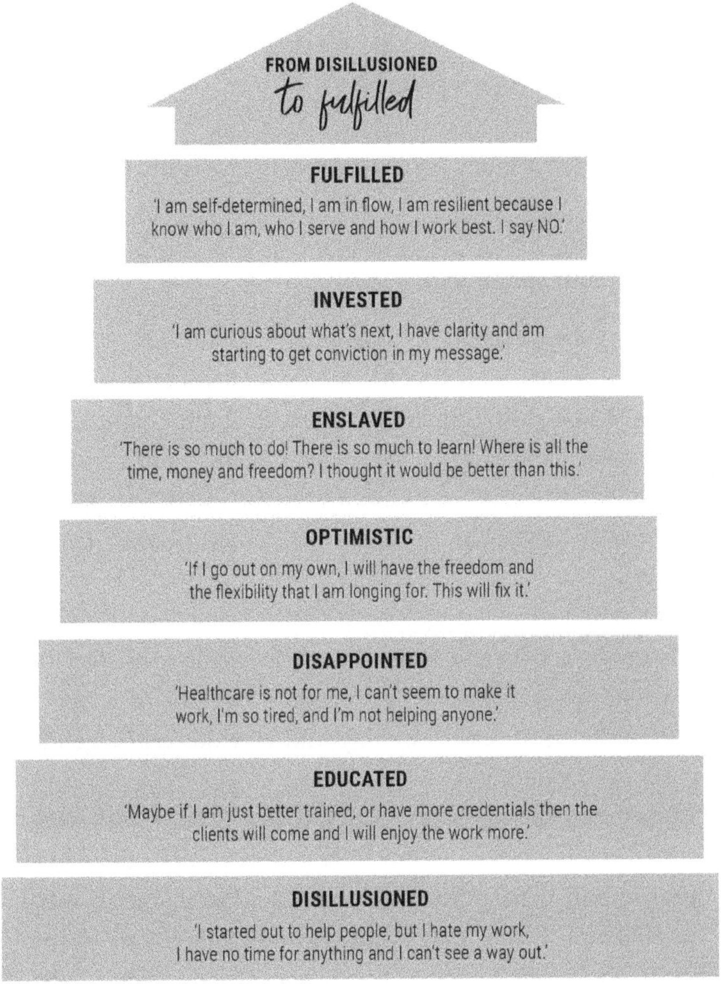

FROM DISILLUSIONED
to fulfilled

FULFILLED
'I am self-determined, I am in flow, I am resilient because I
know who I am, who I serve and how I work best. I say NO.'

INVESTED
'I am curious about what's next, I have clarity and am
starting to get conviction in my message.'

ENSLAVED
'There is so much to do! There is so much to learn! Where is all the
time, money and freedom? I thought it would be better than this.'

OPTIMISTIC
'If I go out on my own, I will have the freedom and
the flexibility that I am longing for. This will fix it.'

DISAPPOINTED
'Healthcare is not for me, I can't seem to make it
work, I'm so tired, and I'm not helping anyone.'

EDUCATED
'Maybe if I am just better trained, or have more credentials then the
clients will come and I will enjoy the work more.'

DISILLUSIONED
'I started out to help people, but I hate my work,
I have no time for anything and I can't see a way out.'

Figure 2.1: From disillusioned to fulfilled

1. Disillusioned

Right now, you feel trapped by a whole host of expectations, no matter whether you're working as an employee or working in your own practice.

You are disillusioned because you have no control over:

- your work load
- your client work
- your weekend because you're exhausted!

When I was disillusioned by my work, I felt conflicted by my desire to help my clients and my frustration with all the rules, structures, systems, and other things that always seemed to make the execution of the work with clients difficult.

My desire to help and make change occur made me feel like I was always banging my head against the bars of a cage. I was working someone else's way with someone else's agenda.

I was told when to come to work, where I could work from, who I would see, how much time as available for which person and what other resources I had available to work with them. I was told what the outcomes with clients needed to be and in what timeframes. It felt stifling, it felt like there was not room for individuals, that everyone had become a part of some big system.

Oh, you feel like this too, huh?

2. Educated

When times are tough, we as health professionals will often ask ourselves: what is wrong with me that I can't make this work? So we think that the answer comes in the guise of more knowledge, more skills and more credentials and initials to our name.

Guilty!

I thought that if I could learn to be a better rehabilitation counsellor by learning more counselling skills then I would be able to get the type of results that I wanted. Then I thought that if I learned Occupational Health and Safety, I would be more respected and be able to have a more significant voice. (I started a graduate Diploma in Occupational Health and Safety three times before I worked out that I did not want to study OH&S.)

This list goes on:

- management skills
- mediation practice
- administration basics…

…on and on it goes…

Sure, while this 'stuff' may be useful it does not fix the problem. In actual fact, it adds MORE to the problem because you lose more time and sleep by cramming even more things into your already bursting schedule!

3. Disappointed

There comes a time for all of us, where we will feel the tensions between caring for people and working in a resource-limited environment. We are disappointed by what feels like lack of professional development, we are disappointed in management and leadership decisions, we are disappointment in government priorities and policy.

At a day-to-day level, most us working on the coal face become disappointed that we can't make 'it' work. That we haven't been able to affect the kind of change that we thought we could.

We know that working harder isn't the answer because it's simply more of the same. People are directing us in ways that don't make sense. We just don't seem to fit!

I have always had a problem with the leadership and management in any salaried position that I was in. I questioned my fit. I decided that there was something inherently wrong with *me* if I could not make being a health professional work because it looked like everyone else could, so it stands to reason then that I was the problem.

Therefore, my solution was to leave the profession altogether. Something that so many health professionals are choosing to do every day, to start their own practice.

4. Optimistic

When I ask health professionals why they want to have their own private practice, the general answer is − for the freedom and for the flexibility. Our disappointment in agency, government or corporations means we are left chasing the feeling of doing good work, and feeling good about the work we do while caring for our financial needs.

If we don't choose to leave the industry or do something else entirely then we begin asking, 'what if I could do this work my way?'

We become optimistic, we know that the way we help our clients does work. We see the change, the transformation, the hope that we bring people and we want more of that. We want more of that over the endless meetings, paper work that doesn't make sense and levels of reporting and bureaucracy that seems to hinder recovery.

We start daydreaming about working our own hours, setting our own pace, only working with the types of clients who make our hearts sing.

We notice that we are not alone, we are encouraged by others who have done this before us, and we start to really hunger for the satisfaction, the freedom and the flexibility that now appears within our reach.

Our optimism keeps growing until we take that leap … however, then we just end up at another crises point …

5. Enslaved

It's really hard to turn away people who are hurting who we know we can help. It's even harder to turn them away when someone tells you that you're the ONLY person who can help.

The more clients you attract, the more you feel good, but also the more you need to fill in paperwork and do bookkeeping, accounting, debt recovery and compliance. It's a vicious cycle that actually lands you right back where you started – disillusioned and feeling like a slave.

This is not freedom at all. This is not why we created a private practice.

This time, however, you think, 'I don't have a boss, or a team leader or a CEO making me miserable, I did this all by myself to myself.' Yikes!

That's when your migraines start (or at least when mine did) and you fail to switch off from the job. All the fears of 'not being good enough' become raging voices yelling at you.

What to do?

6. Invested

When we see or hear the word 'invested' we often think about financial investment, but it means bringing our whole self to our journey and being committed on that path.

When we are providing services to humans in need who are hurting, and we receive money in exchange for our knowledge, skills and capabilities, we become invested. The risks and responsibilities are now bigger now we are out on our own, and the need for personal accountability can at times be overwhelming.

Our conviction in our message, in the help we can provide grows. This is now not just a job, or a career, working with people in this manner is a *calling*.

When we are so convinced that what we can offer is not just needed, but it is necessary, then we start asking questions like:

- What will it take for me to get my message out?

- How can I help more people?

- Who can help me learn what I don't yet know but need to know?

What occurred for me back in 2010 when I invested time, energy, headspace, and money in my first 12-month business coaching program was that I had become open and curious to *possibilities*. I was hungry to learn how to make this thing called private practice work for me.

I had stopped asking, 'what is wrong with me?' and started asking, 'what is the right way for me?'

I have had so many people whose first question on a practice-building consultation call is, 'How much does it cost to work with you?'. I know that if this is the first question they ask then the person is not going to be a good fit for working with me.

The person who automatically asks how much it costs is not invested. If I told them they could have a one-on-one session with me every week, plus unlimited email access, plus access to my mastermind group all for a total of $20, you know what would happen?

- This person would not do any work.

- This person would only turn up when they 'had the time'.

- This person would not take my recommendations or advice seriously.

You cannot grow your private practice and your revenue, unless you invest in it whole heartedly unless you are all-in. Being invested means you will make the time, you will do the work, you will trust the process.

7. Fulfilled

When I set up my practice I was looking for flexibility, which I thought would bring about freedom. But after 12 months of wandering around aimlessly, working in my private practice (rather than on it) I realised that what I was really seeking was a way to do the work that was FULFILLING.

I wanted to wake up every day energised by my work. I wanted to have time off and not feel guilty, to be able to afford things I wanted to buy, to attend training and international conferences that I wanted to attend.

Fulfillment is not found in another modality, a new niche, a VA, a copywriter or changing the word counsellor to coach. No, fulfillment comes from working out, 'what is right for me?'

Fulfilment means that we are resilient. When we are fulfilled we can get back up when we are knocked down. We are confident that if we need to take time out for personal or family reasons, everything will not crumble around us.

A true sense of fulfillment means that you can turn up every day present, fully aware of the needs of your clients, knowing that all your basic needs have been met and that you have all the time, energy and self-care resources you need to be the best person you can be.

When you are free and fulfilled, you are an entrepreneurial clinician, which means you:

- work the hours that work best for you

- help the people you are best suited to serve

- learn the things that light you up

- write the blogs that share your passion

- create an online presence that inspires, affirms and encourages others

- network to serve the room NOT get referrals for new clients

- commit to learning, growing and becoming the best version of yourself you can be.

When we are an entrepreneurial clinician, we have room in our minds and our souls to think and feel things differently. This is when we can contribute to the real and sustainable change in healthcare that we all long for.

This is how we change healthcare, from the inside out.

Where are you now?

So where are you right now? Are you disillusioned by your work or are you free and fulfilled?

My guess is, if you're reading this book, you still have plenty you could do to make life and work better, no matter where you currently are.

When you start to move towards feeling fulfilled by your work, you will notice you:

- stop fearing lack and start seeing opportunities in everything you do

- find work enjoyable, not something you dread

- have more energy, (though you may not feel like you have enough hours in the day to do all the things that excite you)

- have people in your world who will try to keep you safe, suggesting you slow down, play small and 'take is easy'.

- trust yourself and not blame others

- accept that a $0 bank balance does NOT mean you are a failure.

You will become invested – in how you value your time, energy and future.

Invest in your future

Having a thriving private practice is not just about making oodles of money. The money will come as a RESULT of you being invested in YOU – not just your clients, customers or compliance officers who need you to tick boxes.

This is about:

1. Letting go of your need for certainty and embracing curiosity.

2. Letting go of your fear of failure and seeking clarity about what will work for YOU.

3. Having the conviction that you have your own back, and with the right people, tools and resources you can turn this dream, this wishful thinking into your reality.

When you realise that what you are really seeking is fulfillment, not freedom, then your chains will start to loosen.

There will be an incredible sense of flow, of ease in your practice. This feels weird at first because it feels like you are not working hard enough. Then gradually, you see you are doing exactly what you need to be doing, when you need to be doing it, with who you want to do it.

All the crazy noise in your head stops. You cheer on other clinicians in your town who just won a great proposal. You get excited about other people having waiting lists.

Fulfilment comes from doing what it is YOU want to do, with the people YOU want to do it, in the way YOU want to do it.

That's what's at the heart of the entrepreneurial clinician.

Just like there is no right way to treat a client, there is no right way to build a successful practice.

That's why it's important to build a practice that works for you and your unique situation, needs and wants. That's what we'll look at in Part 2.

INTERVIEW
CATHY LOVE
OCCUPATIONAL THERAPIST, AUTHOR, BUSINESS COACH

Cathy is an occupational therapist (OT), a prolific speaker, presenter and trainer who has presented workshops all over Australia and internationally. She also works with allied health professionals who are keen to develop powerful and profitable businesses that create a positive impact on their owners, their teams, and their clients.

One of the things I love about Cathy is her commitment to all of the people she connects with, which means not just her clients, but her clients' families, care givers, and the people who work inside of these health businesses.

As someone who has built her own practice (and sold a business) and helped others build theirs, she really does understand what it takes to create something profitable and sustainable from the inside out.

••

How has being an occupational therapist provided you with a platform to be able to speak, train, mentor and do other things?

Having worked in OT pretty much exclusively with children, teens and adults with developmental disabilities for over 30 years, I've been able to hone this craft of helping people understand who they are and who they want to be and what they need to be doing in life. For me, I still go back and read the work of Mary Law [**www.thecopm. ca/authors/mary-law**] and look at the person and the environment and the tasks, and how those three circles overlap.

The OTs will be dashing to the internet when they hear this, but it just comes back to how humans do stuff in their environment, and the challenges and opportunities that sit between those overlaps. You twist it all together, and twist it out longitudinally over time, and that is a bit of life, a bit of a view of life.

I love the idea that you don't have to be who you are today. You don't have to be that same person next week or the week after, and there is this beautiful opportunity of growth and layering up your brilliance and change.

Can you define to me what you think entrepreneruial means?

This is an evolving piece of thinking for me and it goes into my critical thinking department quite often.

For me at the moment, being an entrepreneur, being entrepreneurial, is all about understanding what people really need, being able to solve problems, and being able to add value by doing as much as I possibly can with as little as possible.

It's a bit of a synthesis, but that's what I'm sitting with at the moment, and I anticipate that it would change, but imagine a world where problems are solved.

We know that global problems aren't going to be solved by governments.

The business and entrepreneurial community is really starting to step in to look at what people need, how they need it, how to add value and solve problems with that lightness of touch and that lightness of resources.

So what opportunities then do we as health professionals have in an age where being an entrepreneur is highly sought after and highly valued?

This is where I fling my arms as wide as I can!

There is so much opportunity out there, and we are only at the very, very start of the whole tech age, so there's monster-sized opportunities for leveraging technology to optimise our own time and productivity.

In my first business we had practice management software from the early 2000s, and it doesn't compare to what's in the market now. I know that software is a couple of thousand bucks a year, whatever it was, but it saved me a salary.

Now when you think about how software, let's just call it all tech, can do your marketing for you, can automate workflow, can bring reports that you didn't even know you needed, can delight clients in ways that you didn't think were possible, so on and so forth. And this is only the stuff that's available now, so when you think about what's commercially available to health, wellness, disability, imagine what's available commercially elsewhere in other sectors, so we'll be seeing that trickle down I hope.

We can also create a much more significant impact with the way we do business, with the way we do work, with the way we do life.

I think for clinicians to be stepping very quickly into telehealth, digital health and that whole experience, both from a business owner's point of view and from a customer's point of view as well. We are going to be seeing a lot more wearable tech, a lot more automation, a lot more artificial intelligence.

If you're sitting there being fearful and cautious and thinking that won't happen to disability or health, it kind of already is. So be curious and ask yourself some questions 'what if' and 'how could I' and 'what difference would it make' or 'what value would that bring', and that gentle kind of sunrise of bringing this stuff into business with that goal of it being valuable to you and your team and your clients.

What are some of the things that come up as most challenging?

I'm going say mindset first.

I am yet to meet an allied health business owner who doesn't have what I describe as a secret squirrel plan for something else tucked away, and I get really interested in terms of why they haven't opened that box and let that genie out yet.

I think a challenge is to dig into your self-worth and dig into your own personal and professional and even business value about this notion of what people need, how you can enhance people's lives and customers' opportunities, and to really attach to those outcomes that you get with your clients.

Otherwise, you're always going be sitting in a place of tension around money and about selling things. To this day I see that as an exchange of value. I give someone something new and interesting and a new skill, or opportunity, or way of thinking, or doing, or being, and they just happen to give me money.

So other challenges include just pulling on your business boots a bit as well. Whether it's your numbers, whether it's getting your marketing mojo up a little bit. Mindset, confidence, risk, knowing your value, knowing your numbers would be challenges that I see that aren't insurmountable.

When you've got time and the right sort of support team in place, and that belief that you're truly, truly worth it, that stuff is workable.

Here is a challenge and an opportunity, and that's about allied health professionals leaning in and not muttering and complaining and whinging to each other about who's not doing what at a professional association level, but actually making some noise.

When looking back now, what would you definitely do differently in starting your business if you were starting today?

I would look at what it would take to build a business that demands less of me.

OTs use the expression 'a million dollar business'. What sort of business model would I need to have to have a role that is team-facing but is a million bucks worth of customer delight? I would work with an advisory crew for startup beforehand, and I would have different sort of product structures in place. The reason being that I'm of the thinking that this notion of one-to-one therapy, the therapist and the patient, client, customer, I think that's fading from our service offer.

I'd build a business model that was set to fly with less of my time, and I would have a much more sophisticated marketing strategy in place for online and offline marketing. I would have a diverse team. I would bring in clinical excellence across a couple of frontiers, and I would bring in business development management and ninja admin support, and we would have tech doing so many aspects of everything that we needed to.

I think that a new build would look very, very different than starting out of the back of my car and community visits and things like that. I would possibly, if I could, spend two, three, four, five times in the planning and go to market with something quite new and novel and hopefully position myself a little ahead of the curve.

What is the number one thing you would encourage any health professionals to do or have who wants to be successful in a clinical career?

I cannot stand the expression 'clinical supervision'. Cannot stand it. What I love to stand in is clinical coaching.

When you're being supervised, you're kind of being told what to do. What this clinical coaching thing gets us thinking about is that both the coach and the coachee are in a position of learning and curiosity and 'what if'. 'Whatifness', as I talk about.

What a coaching approach to clinical performance does is gets the coachee or the therapist doing the mental gymnastics and doing the neural pathways for learning. I don't know about you, but I don't always do what I'm told. It's been on my report since about prep.

I had amazing clinical wisdom in the room in my early clinical positions, but even still, there would be part of me that would do it the hard way just to kind of test some theories. What I love about coaching is the questions:

- What could it look like?

- What would success look like?

- How could you apply that differently?

- Have you seen this before?

- What worked last time?

- What have you done that worked well, how could

you dial that up a bit, or what do you think you need to leave out?

So you're asking all these powerful socratic questions where the coachee has the opportunity to do that clinical reasoning if you like, rather than being told a clinical pathway. Do this and this and this.

To be successful, clinicians need to take pride in being clinicians.

I remember going to an OT conference years and years and years ago, and it was all hail to the researchers, all hail to the academics, and I went nuts just quietly. Absolutely nuts, because I knew, and I was probably one in the audience, that there were clinicians with 20 years of clinical wisdom, and their knowledge wasn't better or worse. It was just different. But for some reason that's not acknowledged on the podium and in the award ceremonies and all of those other things like that. To take pride in the fact that you are carving yourself out for a clinical career. Your professional impact will be different, and it will be vast.

So, what would be the number-one thing that a health professional who wants to be a success in private practice needs to have, or needs to do, or needs to become?

The textbooks would say that you start with the end in mind.

I know I'm not always sure that you know where the end is when you get started, and particularly if you're going into the sort of startup that has a short-term goal. You need a series of projects, a series of sprints to help you feel like you are achieving your goals, and if your business is growing and changing, then you need agility. You need professional, personal, financial, marketing agility around knowing your numbers, knowing what's working, knowing what isn't and changing.

So, the end in mind is really important on a business front, but I think the end in mind is also important on a personal front in terms of whether you're buying yourself a job. Whether you're prepared to be a slave for X number of years. Whether or not you're going get the help you need to really launch with a high sense of personal value, high sense of client value, high sense of impact and all of that sort of stuff. That begs to digging into thinking about the person that you need to be for your business and for your team as well.

Are you big enough in spirit and energy and decision-making and confidence and creativity, and are you big enough in crazy to actually take on this adventure?

Managing your energy, whether it's nutrition, or exercise, or sleep, or hydration, or breath, or whatever it is that brings the best version of you to the day, day after day, day after day, that's the stuff that doesn't hit the business plans. Well it hits the business plans I work on, but I doesn't hit the business plan, and it is often the first to fall. And all of a sudden, the business and the business plan aren't working, but it's actually often interwoven with the business owner and their vibrancy as well, and what they bring to that.

I love the idea that you don't have to be who you are today. You don't have to be that same person next week or the week after, and there is this beautiful opportunity of growth and layering up your brilliance and change.

Part 2

HOW TO BECOME AN ENTREPRENEURIAL CLINICIAN

NOW YOU KNOW WHY YOU ARE disillusioned and feeling trapped by your business or workplace, you are ready to learn how to change that.

Becoming an entrepreneurial clinician is a journey, not a destination. It's a new way of thinking and a way of being.

This is when we start to integrate all of the parts of our work to make it work for us, for our clients and to bring about the change in health and wellness that our communities are hungry for.

In Part 2, we will discover how you can create the work you love, with the people you want to work with, in the way you want to work through three key areas:

1. **Who you are**

   Most clinicians are in such a rush to get new clients in the door they forget the single biggest asset to any health business is YOU – the person providing the service. You need to be clear on who you are and what you offer before anything else.

2. **Who you serve**

   Your clients are not looking to be treated by acronyms or credentials, they want to know YOU CARE. It is your responsibility to find out who you best serve, and who you like to serve, so that you can serve them well.

3. **How you communicate**

   When you know who you are and who you best serve, then you can begin to communicate these things in the best way to your clients. This means online, as well as offline.

Chapter three

Who you are

RACHEL WAS A CLIENT OF MINE who had been in private practice for two years and was stuck. She was struggling trying to work out why she wasn't attracting clients.

Like many others like her, she had:

- a website

- a designer and copywriter

- a business coach

- an electronic health records subscription

- a virtual assistant

- an up-to-date Psychology Today profile

- Google adwords

- regular Facebook and social media content.

Rachel found herself asking why on earth she had invested so heavily in all her years of training, then in all the trappings of a private practice when still she had very few people coming directly to her. (Can you relate?)

When I met Rachel she was burned out, despondent and constantly asking, 'why can't I make this work?' She criticised herself at every turn, 'why can't I do this when everyone else can. What's wrong with me?'

She desperately wanted to experience the lifestyle freedom that she thought would come with running her own practice. She had followed the 'rules' and done some of the work, but where was the choice, the ideal clients, the freedom and laptop lifestyle that she longed for?

I was sad for Rachel, but also relived because what she was experiencing – what you are probably experiencing – is 100% fixable. In my initial one-on-one with Rachel I did an audit of her online presence and realised her image online did not match up to who she was offline.

Rachel was turning people away without realising it – it's likely you are doing this, too.

In person, Rachel was:

- smart – no nonsense, yet compassionate
- opinionated – these opinions were well founded in experience and an evidence-based practice
- savvy – she was an immigrant, a single mum and had embarked on a career in mental health as a purposeful career change
- delightful – she had a lovely accent that added to her uniqueness
- passionate – about people living symptom and pain free.

There was nothing vanilla about Rachel. Yet online, her passion to engage with clients, to make transformational change for people was lost. She knew lots of 'stuff', lots of acronyms patients didn't understand (EFT and EMDR, for example). I as a potential client, could tell she could treat people with anxiety, but I didn't know if I could be classified as 'anxious', so maybe Rachel wasn't for me.

This is such a common mistake. We are so good at listing our qualifications and the modalities that we have trained in, but what we remain poor at communicating is:

1. Hey person who is hurting, can I help you?

2. Here's what I know about what you might be experiencing.

3. Here is how I can help you.

4. Here's how you can get in touch with me.

Rachel was caught in the trap of wanting to 'sell' services that people would buy, rather than offering the service people need that answered their biggest problem right now. If a potential client came to her website at a time when they were hurting, confused and anxious about asking for help, it would not be clear to them how, or even if, Rachel could help them.

If they looked at some of her other listings, such as her Psychology Today and Good Therapy profiles they would be even more confused, because the information on these sites was so different from her website that it was like reading about two different clinicians.

Confused people do not purchase our services –
they run and never come back or stop
seeking help entirely.

Be authentic

Authenticity is the degree to which an individual's actions are congruent with their beliefs and desires, despite external pressures. In other words, being authentic is about being genuine and being real.

It's not about looking like you are living the Instagram life, which we all know is fake, an ideal that we don't have the energy for.

Inauthenticity makes us cringe. It's the kind of behaviour that makes every health professional in the world think, 'please don't make me sell, I'm not a used car sales person.'

So what happens when we experience someone who is not congruent, who is *inauthentic* as a clinician in private practice?

When we meet inauthentic health professionals we
close our eyes and hope they leave us alone.

A lack of authenticity creates a sense of confusion with potential clients, which creates a lack of trust. Trust is one of the most crucial elements in a fruitful clinician–client relationship. If they do not trust you, they do not ask you for help, which means you do not grow a private practice that you are proud of. Period.

When you copy someone else's website copy or Psychology Today profile (c'mon, admit it!) then you are being inauthentic. As soon as someone who has been attracted to you through your website copy (which wasn't really yours and doesn't express who you are) gets to speak to you on the phone they will be suspicious. Even if they can't articulate what's 'wrong' they will be left with a feeling of unease.

Most of us are working with people when they are at an incredibly vulnerable place and time in their life, they do not need more unease, especially from someone they have yet to meet.

It is a privilege to work with people when they are at their most vulnerable, when they are sick, scared, alone, isolated, and confused. They have often never been in this situation before, so they look to us for certainty and for safety.

Build trust, not blanket statements

By the time most of our clients or patients arrive in front of us, they have had their fill of being poked and prodded by medical professionals with no bedside manner, of working with hospital and clinic administrators, insurance companies or funding bodies that refer to them as a number or a diagnosis only.

What they really want is to be assured that they are going to be OK.

They want to know that if they give us their hard-earned (and often fought-for) cash, their limited time, and even more limited energy, then we are going to genuinely help them. They want to know that we will not rip them off. They want to know that we have their back. They want to know that they can TRUST US.

Without trust, clients won't engage you, they won't stick around and they won't continue to exchange their money for your expertise.

When a prospective client reads your online profile and your website and your LinkedIn profile they have formed an impression of you. So if their in-person experience of you isn't the same as their online impression of you, there will be a MASSIVE trust issue.

If they don't trust you, then you never see that client again, and potentially they might stop trying to get help with

ANYONE, not just you, because they don't feel safe. (That, as you know, is a tragedy.)

Our prospective clients really do not care what we have studied or for how long for. They just want to know, 'can you help me? Can you help me to feel better about my diagnoses, fears and concerns? Can you help me feel better with my baggage, my lack of understanding, my self-doubt, skepticism, lack of discipline and my shame?'

The real currency of health is not money, it is trust.

YOU are your best asset

Who you are really matters. As leading speaker Simon Sinek says, 'No one really cares what it is you do, they want to know why you do it and they want to know you.'

You are asking people you have never met, who are scared, often in pain or traumatised, to trust you with their most vulnerable self. Your first responsibility here is to help them understand that you genuinely want to help, and that you will do no harm.

This is not an intellectual construct based on what you know (your credentials).

This is an emotional connection you are creating based on who you are (your authentic self).

When we know the VALUE we bring to our clients then we hold our heads high. We speak with clarity and certainty. We no longer blame the government or the health system for the shortfalls in health service provision, we take a stand and say, 'Hey, if you want to get well, if you want to make change I am here to help you.'

When we start to believe in who we are, then we know that to compare ourselves to other clinicians is not only pointless but also it's self-limiting. When we know who we are and what VALUE we add to our clients, we can walk away from fear of comparison or feeling not up to the job.

There are hundreds of new graduates every single year, but there is only ONE of you doing what you do, the way that you do it with the people you are best positioned to serve, so value that.

Your uniqueness, the WHO YOU ARE of your practice, is your most valuable asset. Yet, it's the thing clinicians often overlook because we have all been taught to follow the rules, the procedures, the process that ensures we comply with our industry and with every one of our peers.

The problem with our profession is everything is set up to make sure we DO NOT stand out.

Putting yourself OUT THERE in a real authentic way, in the real world is scary. It opens you up to peer review, criticism and comparison. I get it.

But NOT putting yourself out there is far worse. After all, how will you ever get to do the work you love with the people you want to help in the way that brings you fulfilment? (That's why you're reading this book, remember.)

Even though it's scary, putting yourself out there is exactly what you need to do to allow your prospective clients to feel like they connect with you, to feel safe and secure with you, to *want to work with you*.

Show you care

Look at it like this, I would expect that a physiotherapist – any physiotherapist – would know what to do if I turned up with a broken bone. However, as a patient, I don't just want my fracture set. I want my fracture set, and I want to feel cared for in the process. I want someone to make sure my pain is OK, that I am given education or instructions to help me manage that pain in the days after the shock has subsided, and some follow-up to keep me on the right track, to feel cared for in my journey to recovery.

I want a LOT more than just setting a broken bone, don't I?

One of the most gratifying statements I hear time and again from my clinical and coaching clients is, 'Wow Jo, you really do care'. Yes, I do – and it's sad that my clients are always so surprised at this.

It shouldn't come as a surprise that a health professional actually cares about their clients and their wellbeing – yet it does.

Following processes and rules and doing what we know works are all important, especially at the beginning of our clinical work when we need to be heavily reliant on the processes, until they become second nature. However, that does not mean we need to become clones of our peers or of the people who have taught us the processes.

This is an all-too-frequent problem. We can be so busy fulfilling someone else's version of who we are, that we forget who we *actually* are.

If you don't tap into what makes you unique, you will end up with a boring and beige website, a LinkedIn profile that is like every other clinician out there, and something that does not even vaguely reflect the real you.

Who you are as a clinician – how you treat patients as people, how you manage their fears and concerns – matters even more than what you actually do in your role as a clinician.

People treat people

Think about every time you have been a patient. Above all else, what is it that you wanted to *feel* after your interaction or treatment?

You wanted to feel cared for.

This is why I will travel up to two hours in peak-hour Sydney traffic to see the right rheumatologist. Why I will travel an hour to see a counsellor I like, and why I will pay my nutritionist up to six months' of service in advance. I want the people who care for me to be in my world.

People want to be treated and served by the people they know, like and trust.

When we reduce our knowledge, skills and expertise to a set of processes and systems, then prospective clients do not see OUR uniqueness and humanness and they simply do the smart thing – ask us to compete on price. After all, when we are coming to the market as a credential, a qualification, a set of systems and processes that each and every other clinician has, we create a LOT of competition.

No one else can do this work quite the way you can. No one else can offer the insights and lessons the way you can. You may be THE only person who creates the opportunity for real and lasting change with your client, where so many other health professionals have tried and failed.

Like you, I was taught to leave my emotions at the door when I arrived at work. I was taught NEVER to share a personal experience with a client in case it confuses the client–clinician professional ethics and boundaries. I was told to always go back to the process if I got stuck.

Being clinically sound is no longer enough. Our prospective clients expect that if we have a qualification, a credential and a license to practise that we actually know what we are doing.

Our competence is not the point of difference – it's actually a given, the expected, the baseline. Our point of difference is how we do the work.

Get clear on who you are

Whoever said that starting, building and running your own business is the biggest self-development journey you will ever go on was completely right.

Every time I sit down to review my web copy, I engage in a discussion with myself around who I want to be. I reflect on whether I am currently working in a way that says I am this person. EVERY SINGLE TIME.

Every time I am asked to submit a bio for a speaking engagement or a podcast interview, I step back and ask, does this reflect who I am and not just what I do? EVERY SINGLE TIME.

Looking at your online copy is the wrong place to start.

*The right place to start is becoming clear about
who you are — as a person, a clinician and
a helper and healer.*

An acquaintance once shared with me their experience of searching for an OT. He was not a health professional and had not ever heard of this thing called OT until he was advised to consult one.

His questions included:

- What is an OT, is this a type of medical device?

- How do I find one?

- What do I ask for?

- Do I really need this?

- What can they do that my doctor can't?

- I already have a physiotherapist, a GP, a dietician and a personal trainer, why do I need another person to help me?

Anyone can shop online for an OT. Anyone can shop online for an OT specialising in adults with spinal cord injuries. However, the issue is that most of the population cannot tell you what an OT does.

*It is the human behind the jargon that they
are buying into.*

One of the challenges we as clinicians experience here, is that we must become qualified, licensed, credentialed and supervised before we can practise. So, we can be forgiven for thinking that our clinical skills are the sum total of what we have to offer our clients.

Yet, who we are is more than just a function of our personality. It's much more than a wish list of characteristics that we would like to have that we think might be attractive to others.

This is an exploration that includes our:

- personality
- behaviours
- natural skills and abilities
- personal likes and dislikes
- strengths and weaknesses.

This is why the next exercise may not be easy. But it is necessary.

If you don't know who you are and what on earth it is you stand for you, you will not be able to market yourself and will not build something that is fulfilling for you.

What do you really want?

First up, it is completely OK for you to want things!

It's completely OK to want good health, a happy and cohesive family, to want to travel the world, to have an exciting and profitable business, to have all the time energy and resources that you need to live the life you want.

IT'S OK TO WANT ALL OF THOSE THINGS.

You are not selfish, you are not inconsiderate, you are not egotistical, you are not going to be punished.

> *You need to get rid of any false guilt and assumptions you have made about not being good enough or worthy enough to have the things you want.*

I meet so many people who have a fear of wanting. I know this fear, because it was mine too – I was fearful of being labeled as selfish, materialistic, money driven, I was afraid people (especially my family) would reject me, that friends would want to take advantage of me ... after all, who am I to 'be' anyone; what makes me so special?

> *You also need to let go of the goals, hopes and dreams that others have imposed upon you.*

You know: our parents, our children, our best friends, our pastors, our ex partners, our current partners ... we can find a really long list of people to blame here, but that's not helpful. It is time to grow up and become accountable for those things we really want.

If guilt and shame or some kind of trauma is keeping you from expressing your own desires, then please seek professional help before moving onto the next section.

What I would like you to do is answer these questions honestly:

1. How old will you be in five years' time?

2. What did you expect you would be doing by that age?

3. What things did you expect to have in your life by then?

4. What things did you vow you would NOT be doing by then?

5. Can you see the pathway to make your life five years from now happen?

We are starting five years into the future because we want to work back from something meaningful. Remember this is no longer about wishful thinking. No longer about someone else's goals and vision for your life. This is YOUR life.

Write down in your journal or in the notes section provided in the back of this book, in as much detail, everything you can about your five years into the future self. You can use single words, phrases, prose, pictures, stories, feelings, emotions, sensations, and experiences to help you.

This is a brain dump. It is not about analysing whether any of this is possible or not, so let yourself go.

Next, you will bring this future into the present.

Ask yourself:

1. What three words do I hear people use to describe me frequently (e.g. patient, loving, kind, bossy, opinionated, caring, brave)?

2. What am I currently known for?

3. What do I want to be known for?

4. What are the three most important things that I could NOT live without (e.g. family, friends, coffee, travel, freedom, choices, money)?

5. What five things do I LOVE about my work and life to date?

6. What five things about my work do I NEVER want to do again?

7. What really annoys me and makes me so mad I want to scream?

8. What makes me sad?

9. What makes my heart sing, what lights me up?

Now, I want you to have a good look at your answers:

1. What have you learned about yourself that you did not know before you did this exercise?

2. What parts of who you are have you rejected or been embarrassed by?

3. What parts of you form the essence of the person you want to be?

I did this exercise with my client Pete, a professional counsellor and coach and an all-round nice guy who was part of my Accelerate Your Practice Program. Pete had recently been offered what felt like an incredible opportunity: to become a salaried employee within a local business that sounded just like the type of business he wanted to create.

His rationalisation was that he should postpone his dream of growing his own business for a while, until he had some experience inside a business that was similar to what he wanted to build.

That's some pretty cool logic and a great way to feel safe. However, Pete was 30 at the time and he thought he would spend the next two years as an employee.

Now I know from experience that it takes about two years to become comfortable in your own skin after leaving a salaried position, given that you have to un-learn how to be an employee, learn how to market and sell YOU and YOUR service, manage your own bookkeeping and the seemingly endless list of to-dos that happen when you're in business for yourself. Yes, you might be making good money, but it takes a lot of energy and effort in this two-year period.

So that would bring Pete up to being 34 years of age. So, I asked him, 'what did you think your life would be like by 35 years? Did you want to be an ex-employee in a startup phase, or did you have something else envisioned for your life?'

This was the turning point for Pete. Once this question was put to him, the answer became easy. No way did he want to 'gift' two years (or more) of his life to build someone else's business, just so he could feel safe. By 35 he wanted marriage, kids and a sense of something growing.

The decision was made – now was the time to put into place those things that would lead to his vision of 35. He focused on the goals he had set for himself, knowing who he was and what he wanted, and as a result, in the following 12 months, Pete went from around $50Kpa, to over $120Kpa in his practice.

*That is the power of owning who you really are
and what you really want.*

Reframe and reset

Now if you have never done an exercise like this before you might find this confronting. Sometimes it really hard to see the good in the way we describe ourselves and we are left feeling, 'Yuck, I don't want to be this person.'

Remember, this is an exercise in self-awareness. The purpose of this is to empower us to grab a hold of our uniqueness, to own it and to celebrate it. This means the ugly bits too.

As an example, when I do this exercise on myself. I hear the following words as the ways people have described me:

- bossy
- intolerant
- arrogant
- impatient
- selfish.

As I type these words I find myself slumping my shoulders, grimacing and feeling less than. I don't like those words and I don't want to be those words. However, there is some truth to them. Yet, in the right context, this can be flipped to become incredibly empowering.

My business mentor Janine Garner helped me to own these elements of myself by reframing what I saw when I described myself:

- bossy – REFRAME TO ambitious, committed to success

- intolerant – REFRAME TO accountable, conscientious

- arrogant – REFRAME TO certain

- impatient – REFRAME TO driven

- selfish – REFRAME TO holds great boundaries.

I know I'm ambitious, but not at any cost. I don't let ambition get in the way of relationships with people I love. I know that some people can find me frightening and scary, however they understand that's because I won't let them make excuses. I am a strong implementer and hold people to a high standard. This might feel arrogant, but in all honesty I think we can do better in the healthcare sector. I believe it's NOT OK that people don't get the healthcare they need.

So, here's your challenge:

- Where you see 'impatience', what might others see?

- Where you see 'slow to change', what might others experience?

- Where you see 'unable to make a decision', what do others say?

It is only by doing this exercise that we start to own who we really are. It is only when we own who we really are, that we can communicate that to others in an authentic and congruent way.

You are not stuck in an institution.

You are not beige and you are not grey.

You do not have to fit in the box.

You can be YOU.

And you can do that very well.

> *Own who you are because that will help you determine who you are best able to serve.*

Who you serve is what we will look at in the next chapter.

INTERVIEW
JEFFERY JENKINS
PODIATRIST, CO-DIRECTOR –
ONE POINT HEALTH

Jeff is a podiatrist with a vision of how patients (clients) can receive better services. That led to him creating a large multidisciplinary allied health practice in the west of Sydney, currently with two sites and plans for more.

One of the remarkable things about Jeff is how he has collaborated with like-minded people to build something unique yet powerful for the people who need their services.

I've been watching the development of One Point Health closely (as they are located in my local community), and I've seen firsthand how their influence in the community has increased. In preparation for this interview, I found myself comfortably enjoying the One Point waiting area, where I observed many happy people – both staff and clients.

We often hear as health professionals, that bigger is not always better, but Jeff provides some insights into mindset, and how we address fear and the value of consistency, which I'm now keen to put into practice within my own work.

••

Can you describe the entrepreneurial journey of One Point?

We initially had three podiatry clinics in Penrith, all owned by separate people. About five years ago, my business partner and I were tinkering around with looking at expanding or moving to a new site. By chance, we met with another podiatry practice owner in the area at an education event and we got talking with them. They were probably our biggest competitors, but we were having a chat about our desires to get bigger and to grow, and the next thing you know we're developing Western Sydney Sports Medicine and that was the first go at this multi-disciplinary centre. Two years after that we said, 'You know what, let's bring all the centres together. Close them down, bring them all together and just start one big amalgamation.'

That led to One Point Health. One Point Health then moved on to purchase a physiotherapy clinic which has also been in the region for 20-plus years and then we went on to purchase Ryde Podiatry Clinic after that as well.

It was a pretty scary time for us. A lot happened in a very short period of time. But before the actual acquisition occurred we took the time to develop a relationship with the other podiatry clinics.

We looked at our competitors as an opportunity rather than as a direct competitor.

This helped us move away from our fears of what if they do us wrong? Or what if we do them wrong by accident? It was important for us to uphold our integrity during this process.

We each had many years of growth and many years of practising in the local region as single operators. I think that was a huge entrepreneurial move on both parts.

I feel like when you can seek out and take risk in developing what we call meaningful like-minded relationships with meaningful like-minded people then there's plenty of opportunities.

How does entrepreneurial thinking help us as health professionals?

It's really a tough question but I'll try to break it down. I think there is a huge amount of opportunities in health to start with in Australia. It's one of the strongest industries that has less of an impact from the world economic trends and movements. I think from the outset there's huge opportunity there.

I think from the clinical side of things, touching on what I mentioned before, it's about working together with people and developing really meaningful valued relationships. One of the biggest things for us was to bring many professions together rather than have isolated professions in different areas. For example, podiatry in one building that was in South Penrith and physiotherapist on another building in the CBD of Penrith. Our thinking was to bring everyone together to build those personal relationships between practitioners because a lot of the clinical evidence says that you have improved business outcomes and health outcomes when you work together as a team.

When you work together as a team, that will also make it a lot more convenient for the patients. The patients, and people in general, are time poor these days. So, by creating convenience and creating better health outcomes there's a real crossover there between the business and the clinical sides.

Everything's so fast these days and what I mean by fast is everything is accessible at a drop of a hat. So if someone walks in off the street, wanting to book an appointment with a podiatrist, but they are booked out for the day, then it's easy for them to walk out the front door. There's no opportunity there to regain that patient or that client. Everything's immediate, everything's so fast. If we can capture that and really focus on the convenience side of things I think that's a big opportunity there for many health practitioners.

This has been a huge thing for us. Developing protocols and processes so we could then one (1) make One Point scalable but also have two (2) consistent service. I remember reading something by the ex-marketing director of Coca-Cola before he moved to Airbnb and one of the biggest things he said was that the biggest downfall for businesses, particularly small to medium sized businesses who want to go to that next stage in growth, is creating consistency in your services and your products. For example, wherever you go in the world when you walk into McDonalds you get the same experience every single time.

So for us, protocols and processes that were scalable, that were obviously taking into account not losing that personal touch from going small to medium, was a huge factor for us. It was really something we put a lot of time and effort into.

What do you think are some of the biggest challenges that clinicians face these days?

Fear of failure and what other people think, fear of what I'm going to think of myself. It's a huge reason why people don't take risks. It's because they scared of what could possibly happen.

I think that's a major factor and I think for myself moving on from when I first came out of uni and wanted to get into the podiatry world and I've always wanted to have my own podiatry practice or be involved in some sort of partnership. I think a major way to assist yourself to get over that fear is just surround yourself with really positive people. Surround yourself with the people who are constantly pushing themselves to do better. Who are going to influence you in a really positive way, who are happy to mentor, happy to give advice. Whether the advice is great or shocking but it's still experience and advice.

In health, there is also a stigma for making money from patients with injuries. I think there's a grey area. It's only grey because as health practitioners you generally go into health to help people. I've always thought that if you're good at what you do in providing good service you don't have to worry about that stigma because you're successful for a reason.

When you're successful for providing good service, for being good at what you do, then that will overcome the stigma and fear of going bigger and not looking like you're taking advantage of patients who are in pain.

After all, what does too big mean? Does too big mean that you lose that personal touch? You lose that real individualised service but I think if you implement those processes and you have a good foundation or baseline values of putting the patient first then I think there's very little chance of losing that personal touch. And again, it's about constantly getting that feedback and constantly reflecting on what you're doing and whether you're doing enough to make sure you're upholding those good meaningful relationships with patients.

That's why it's important to have a good life balance between business and the clinical side of things. One of the reasons I feel we've been somewhat successful over the last three years is one of the first things we did as directors was to cut down our clinical time. We immediately cut our clinical days down to two days a week in order to give ourselves time, because when you have time, you have time for your creativity and your opportunity to think in an entrepreneurial way of thinking. When you don't have time, when you're stressed, you just don't think.

I have to say this point was one of the most difficult things for us because there was an immediate impact and a direct impact in our revenue. We were all booked out. Booked out for weeks and weeks. Therefore, to cut our time to see patients was an immediate reflection on revenue and some patients weren't happy about it either.

They're the risks that you have to take in order to give yourself time to make entrepreneurial decisions, to keep moving forward, keep growing and providing a positive environment for your patients and for your staff.

What do you think the number-one thing is that any new clinician needs to be successful in?

What comes to mind is the good old cliché: hard work, but I really think there's a lot more to it. I really think there is some key points that will get you much further both from a clinical and a business perspective.

Learn to develop, value and grow meaningful interpersonal relationships because without those from a clinical perspective, patients won't feel that they can trust you.

I'm in my early 30s now and from a practitioner point of view for someone to pay $180 or whatever that's a lot of money to see a young person. So you need to have the ability to develop trust for that patient or for that patient to trust you within the first 30 seconds they meet you. To build that trust initially for a patient and then to be able to maintain it I think is a very important.

I reckon 90% of our opportunities from a business perspective come from developing relationships, maintaining them, making sure you don't just forget about the ones that haven't really eventuated as something really successful or beneficial for you. It's a huge reason why I feel like we're very well known in our community, because we cherish those relationships. They're so important. We've been in the area for 35 years and if you forget about your relationships then opportunities simply dry up.

We just don't get taught this at uni. I think it's a very difficult and time-consuming skill to develop. And it's funny, when we do interviews for new practitioners or admin staff, the first thing we look at is the type of person they are. We don't care about what people's scores are in their academic study.

We look at what type of person they are, how they are going to be interacting with other staff in their team and, most importantly, their patient.

Chapter four

Who you serve

AT MY PRACTICE, PURPLECO, I have the privilege of working alongside some incredible clinicians. One of them (let's call her Lucia) is a talented social worker who can work with clients in tough situations.

She helps homeless clients living with brain injuries who often need to attend court. Accessing accommodation, food and medical services is her gift. I am in awe of her.

As a part of our work together she accepted a referral from me for a pregnant young mother of two children who lives with a debilitating chronic illness. A bio-psycho-social screen from me indicated that Lucia had the knowledge skills and experience to help this new client.

Lucia to her credit, tried everything known to humankind. She engaged in text conversations when the client refused to get on the telephone, she engaged the funding body when the client had questions about participation expectations, she even went to visit the client on a weekend so that she could receive services. Lucia really went above and beyond to try to help this young woman.

This went on for a few months, until one day I received a call from Lucia who was rather despondent. She expressed that she had failed me and failed the client and didn't think she could do this work anymore. I was so shocked. Here I was telling the world about this incredible woman on my PurpleCo team, and here she was sounding flat, over functioning and trying to prove to me that she was no longer any good at this work. It took me a few moments to realise what had occurred.

No one had done anything wrong – it was just the wrong client–clinician fit.

This wrong fit was creating so much angst that it led Lucia to think that she had failed, and that she needed to cease doing the work she loved and was so good at.

Lucia is not alone.

Think about the last time you were listening to a client or patient, maybe it was the second or third time you'd met this person, and you had this nagging feeling in the pit of your stomach that something wasn't quite right. You're working hard to be present, you are saying all the right things, making all the right recommendations, yet you still feel 'wrong'.

Suddenly, it hits you – 'This client isn't right for me'.

As health professionals we usually say to ourselves, 'Oh no, I'm not the right fit *for this client*', not the other way around. Not being the right fit for a client often creates a fast downward of emotions and self-doubt:

- Am I doing the right things?

- Will the client get what they need from me?

- What if I'm not good enough?

We start second guessing our competence and then many of us will actually over function, like Lucia did, putting the needs of her client before her own, creating a whole new set of problems for herself:

- losing sleep

- questioning her capability

- feeling like she could no longer do this work

- resenting this client and the work

- burning out.

Over functioning is something that we as high achievers tend to do when we meet someone who is under functioning. We step in to the fill the gap in an effort to help people, which happens a lot of the time because that is our job!

The issue is that we are all taught, regardless of what discipline we might practise on a daily basis, that we serve absolutely everyone. Our qualifications, our credentials and our licenses suggest we can serve anyone who needs help, however, the question is:

Should we serve them just because we can?

Not every client is the right client

Another PurpleCo consultant, Belinda, called me in a fit of frustration one day. She was struggling with a client and was questioning her competence, if she was still able to 'cut it' in the industry.

'You don't have to like every single one of your clients Belinda,' I responded.

That was like music to her ears! She explained that she had never experienced such a strong negative reaction to a client before and prided herself on how she was non-judgmental and able to work with pretty much anyone. However, there were things about this particular client that really upset her, which lead to conflicted values.

Working with this post-motorcycle-accident client triggered really strong emotions for her because she had a family member die in a motorcycle accident. I explained to Belinda that we would simply transfer this client to another clinician, so that she could work with clients that were a much better fit for her – that she didn't have to work with this kind of circumstance.

Saying no is perfectly OK.

I have learned that I am not a good match for:

- people living with addictions
- people who have worked in corrections
- teenage and young adult men.

I know I can work with these clients and do a good job, but I find it very hard. It is not a natural fit for me and I don't enjoy it as much as I do other types of work and people. There are other clinicians out there, however, that I know shine in this area of work and these are the people who I refer these types of client onto.

The work we do is hard enough without having to make it even harder.

If, however, an ex-CEO with a history of cardiovascular disease and major depression who is questioning why he has worked so hard for the last 40 years comes to me, then I know this person is for me to help.

The 27-year old university graduate now living in a power wheelchair as a quadriplegic who has decided he wants more from his life than to game 24/7 – this person, I know is for me.

The therapist who has been working in offshore detention for three years, who has seen the worst of humanity and now needs to integrate back into our wealthy western society – this person, I know is for me.

Our education, our training and our perceptions of client expectations have created a myth that we should serve all the people with all the problems, all of the time.

This is not just untrue, it's also not smart.

*It's not healthy and it's not sustainable for us as
individuals in the healthcare industry to try
and be all things to all people.*

A healthy fit

When we continually work with clients who are not a good
fit for us, we try to over compensate and do things similar
to Lucia at the start. This kind of action is not sustainable.

*If you do not look after yourself and your own
needs first then you actually stop serving
your clients as well.*

When we do this, we interrupt a client's pursuit of
independence and learning because we tend to 'do it all'
for them. Or we go to the other extreme and disengage,
stop caring and start giving a level of care than ticks the
boxes and gets the client out the door in time for the re-run
of *Game of Thrones*.

The longer we work with people who are not a good fit
for us, the more and more reinforcement we receive that
we are not good enough. Our confidence erodes. We stop
feeling energised to go to work. We blame the work, the
industry, the government and then we decide we're not cut
out for it and leave.

*When we don't enjoy working with clients then
we consistently reinforce one of our biggest
fears as a clinician: 'I am not good enough
and someone is going to find out!'*

As clinicians in private practice, who we serve is a vital part of how we care for ourselves and our clients. When we start losing control and feeling like we are not making a difference in our work, we are at risk of burn out.

As clinicians in our own private practices, we actually get to *choose* who it is we want to work with. This might seem like a revelation at first, but it is true and it is a process. You don't magically wake up one day with a caseload full of people you love. (If you have achieved this, however, can you please get in touch with me because I want to learn how you did that.)

*Who we serve is integral to our self-care, to our
ability to experience freedom and fulfillment –
it's our choice.*

Who is your ideal client?

I know what you're thinking. 'OK, that's great Jo, I get I need to find the right clients for me, but how on earth do I do that? And how do I do that *now*?'

But don't be too impatient to get to the 'tell me what to do stage'. First you need to get a good grasp on WHY we are doing this and how you use the information once you have gathered it.

Attracting the right clients is an exercise you have to undergo, it is not a shopping list.

There are some key rules you need to follow and understand before you complete the next exercise.

Your ideal client:

- Is a profile of a person who embodies the attributes of someone you would enjoy working with, who has *problems* you enjoy solving.

- May or may not be a real person.

- *Creates a framework* for you to build your stories, your content, your marketing around. This framework allows you to speak to someone, to create a sense of personal connection rather than a bland third person experience of words that become meaningless.

- May be a combination of many different types of people.

- Will not magically turn up in your schedule just because you have completed an ideal client exercise.

- Is ABOUT YOU just as much as it is about THEM. (Yeah I know, that's a surprise isn't it.)

- Is just that: an IDEAL.

- Will change over time, this is not a set-and-forget exercise.

The purpose of identifying your ideal client is to help you step into the heart and mind of your potential client so that you can let them know that you get them and you are there to help because:

- a confused prospective client will not buy your services

- a prospective client who does not 'know' you will not buy your services

- a prospective client who does not 'like' you will not buy your services

- a prospective client who does not 'trust' you will not buy your services.

A prospective client **will buy your services** when:

- they feel like you understand them

- they feel heard

- they can trust that you are real and authentic.

The purpose of the ideal client exercise is to learn how to communicate with people you can help, in a way that allows them to experience you, like you and trust you.

... And how do you attract them?

There are three steps you need to follow to create the right, and attractive, rapport, both online and offline with the people who you are best able to serve:

1. Identify 150 things about the client you love to serve. (Yep, 150!)

2. Speak to their problems.

3. Write their story.

Let's explore each step in detail.

Step 1: Identify 150 things about the client you love to serve. (Yep, 150!)

Too many health professionals have very little idea about the person they actually want to serve. You need to know your clients better than they know themselves, which is why it's not enough to identify just 10 things about that person.

We are excellent at explaining how to treat a disorder or a diagnosis, but we are terrible at talking to the person who is living with the disorder.

You need to identify 10 things under each of the following subheadings:

1. What their age and income is (demographics).

2. Where they live, what type of living arrangements they have.

3. What their occupation is.

4. What is MOST important to them, what they can't live without.

5. What they like.

6. What they dislike.

7. What they read.

8. What they watch.

9. What social media platforms they use and why.

10. What their self-talk is like.

11. What they are feeling before they meet you.

12. What they are feeling after they have worked with you.

13. What their life will be like if they don't change.

14. What their life will be like if they do change.

15. How they want to make change happen.

When you write things down, they may sound a little repetitive and that is fine. As health professionals we need this because we always fall back into clinical speak. Part of the magic of this exercise is getting you to *think* and *feel* like your client, instead of the clinician who will be treating the client.

Make sure you write using the language your ideal client would use when speaking to you.

What my ideal prospective clients will say is:

> 'Jo, I am so scared, I'm so tired, and I don't know if I can keep going. Is there someone who can help me, and what if this doesn't work. I can't believe I'm 45 years of age and feel like I have to start my career all over again. It's all too hard I wish someone could help me.'

When I do this exercise with my coaching clients, we actually conduct interviews with people who could be their ideal client or who knows the ideal client really well. We write down their exact words (no interpretation, no paraphrasing, no diagnosing) and then look for the common threads in their answers.

So think about previous sessions you have held with clients or start paying attention to what your clients say when they come to see you!

Step 2: Speak to their problems

Once you have done this, then you are ready to identify their biggest problems so you can help solve them. This is about capturing in their own words how they are feeling.

You need to write six to seven statements under each of these headings. I've put in some examples.

1. **Self-talk**

   I'm so fat. I'm so tired. This isn't going to work for me. Everyone is better than me. What if I can't make this work? My reputation is going to be ruined when people find out…

2. **Future**

   I can't go on living like this. What if this only gets worse? Will I really lose my job? What if he/she leaves me? What if I never have kids? I can't do this any longer…

3. **Dreams**

   I wish there was a way I could make this all better. I wish someone would just love me. I hope that I am loveable. It would be so nice to not have to work. Can I just marry someone who will look after me…

4. **Money**

   Making money is so hard. I can't get out of debt. Why does everyone else seem to have it together? Will I ever be able to buy a house? It's easy for them, they have a partner who earns good money…

5. **Career or business**

   I've worked so hard for all these credentials I deserve better. If I can't get this promotion I'm done for. Have I really wasted 20 years of my life with this company? This felt like a good idea at the time, I didn't know it would be this hard. Work is all consuming, I can't do anything but work...

6. **Health**

   When I have more time I will go to the gym. Don't tell me I need to exercise tell me how to find the time. Healthy eating yeah sure, when I'm not so tired. I know I need to prioritise my own health but how when I'm so busy? It's time to look after me. I can't keep looking after everyone else when I have nothing left to give...

7. **Soul**

   I have no peace anymore. I'm worn out on the inside. I can't tell you the last time I laughed. I'm scared of the darkness that is around me.

8. **Relationships**

   I love my friends and my family but I don't seem to be able to keep up with everything. I wish someone would just support me. My partner doesn't understand. My partner just nags me; I don't want to go home. I'm scared that this will tip my partner over the edge and they will leave.

This is about getting into your clients' shoes, about using the language that they use. This is what will help you to craft messages that really speak to the heart of their problems.

Step 3: Write their story

What do you do with all of this awesome information – and these very long lists?

You write your ideal client's story.

This is for YOUR purposes ONLY. This doesn't get published anywhere. Its intention is to allow you to be so comfortable and familiar with your client and their journey that the next time someone asks who you work with, you know exactly what to say.

The easiest way I have found to help my coaching clients begin this story writing process is to ask:

What is your ideal client's problem and how would you respond to their fears?

Problem example:

> Brian is feeling scared and helpless after a heart attack. He is terrified that it will happen again, and so sacred of going back to work in case it happens there. *What if he isn't as good as he used to be? What if all the stress causes another heart attack? What if he can't make his quarterly bonuses and more?*

Response example:

> Brian, I know it's frightening but your fears make a lot of sense to me. Let me work with you and

help you map out the best way to use the energy you have during your day. Sure, it might mean starting off slowly and building up your tolerance to work, but isn't than better than you jumping in and failing?

I'll be here right beside you. I can't tell you how long this will take because this is about you. So, we are going to work this out together. It won't be rushed, you won't feel pushed. I am a resource for you. Helping people to return to work following injury and illness is my zone of genius, I've been doing this a long time, but Brian, I am not an expert in you – so I'm going to need your help as much as you will need me.

Your ideal client story doesn't have a word count, it is as long as you need it to be. Remember, the purpose is NOT to publish this anywhere, but to ensure that you can think and feel your prospective client's thoughts and feelings. If that takes you 10 pages, then that is what it takes. (The first story I wrote was 10 pages long. Now that I've learned to let go of clinician speak I've got them down to about five pages.)

When done properly with the right intention this simple exercise in understanding your ideal client is powerful.

Market yourself, not your services

In the last chapter we focused on the necessity of knowing who you are, and in this chapter we have uncovered the purpose and power of knowing who you serve.

The exercises you've just completed are the foundation to communicating with your ideal clients, which we will look at next in Chapter 5.

You cannot do this properly until you know your prospective clients better than they know themselves. You want them to like you, to want to know you and most importantly you need them to trust you. You are asking people to come and bare their soul, their fears and biggest pain points to you when they have no clue who you are, so it is unfair to ask them to turn up and pay you just because you happen to think you are worth it.

One of the biggest differences between a clinician and an entrepreneurial clinician, is that the entrepreneurial clinician will let their prospective clients know how much they care, how much they get them BEFORE they have sat in a room with them and WELL before the client has paid any money.

When we communicate ourselves with a solid foundation of who we are and who we serve, then we start to attract the right people and we know the people to leave alone.

You will have the confidence to say, 'This is who I am, this is how I serve and this is what I expect from you if we are going to work together'.

That is when you start to do the work you love, the way you love to do it, with the people you are best able to serve.

When you work like this you will let go of 'comparisonitis' and fear of lack. In fact you will be happy to help those who are not a good fit for you find the right practitioner for them.

So clients get the right intervention, with the right person at the right time.

You are healthy and cared for.

Your clients are healthy and cared for.

THIS is how we change healthcare from the inside out.

Now we know who you are and who you best serve, then, and only then, can we start to look at how you best communicate that to others, onto Chapter 5.

INTERVIEW
ANASTASIA MASSOURAS
CEO AND FOUNDER OF PURE INSIGHTS

As the CEO (aka Chief Troublemaker) of Pure Insights, an allied health employment services agency, Anastasia is not your average psychotherapist. You might describe her as a 'silent achiever' for she has grown this solo influential practice to a global team of 145 people who are all dedicated to excellence.

Anastasia is incredibly passionate about closing the gaps in service delivery and is driven to support her team in developing and implementing tailored and high-quality servicing across the board. It's through this that she helps serve some of the most disadvantaged people in our community and cultivates a culture of 'How do we serve?' within her team, which is what I admire most about her.

....

What was it that made you go, 'I want to start my own business?' How did that come about?

It wasn't a conscious decision. It was something that I fell into 16 years ago. Through passion, connection and working with really vulnerable clients in disadvantaged demographics, I saw the impact that genuine care and authenticity can have in the therapeutic process.

It just lit me up and before I knew it I was going from different location to different location doing some really high-level critical work.

One day, I got to a crossroads.

I started questioning *how* I was doing *what* I was doing. (You needed a lot of energy to do the type of work I was doing.) So, I had a decision to make. I couldn't give 200% to every single person walking through the door. So I needed to bring a secondary person on. The question was how do I do that? How do I do that with the absolute belief and trust that the person would care as much as I did and make sure every single client was blessed with the highest quality care?

I would say this is where my entrepreneurial journey started. Then it just organically evolved on its own through the years from there. So, we went from site by site, to region by region, to state by state, until we were servicing nationally and now internationally.

About six years ago, I fell into the work we're doing now in the corporate sector. The Employee Assistance Program is about being passionate about making sure everybody's 100,000 waking hours that are spent at work are spent connected, safe and happy.

But again, it wasn't an initial plan. It was something that we went through with the authenticity and genuine care for what we were doing. We very quickly saw the impact of that process and the support that we were implementing into work places.

How do you live out the values you express within your business?

I think having a very strong connection and attachment to purpose. I'm absolutely unapologetic for that on every single layer.

Also, being very real, so when we put advertisements out there and we invite people in for an interview, it's even to the point of actually trying to talk that person out of the role to show how much we actually genuinely care.

We talk from a value-based connection not just 'great, we can tick a box because you've got the qualification, you've got your association membership and you've got your insurances.'

What does entrepreneurialism or being an entrepreneur mean to you?

Connecting the right people with your mission and your values and having them all in alignment as to where you're going, and why you're going there.

This is not just because we have an organisation and we need to meet X amount of expectation, whatever you set that to be. It's about the bigger impact and the ripple effect of the blessed position we're all in as clinicians to really connect, impact and shift lives. It's one life initially with that individual person you're connecting with, but then it's all the connections that person then has and all the layers of that. So ultimately you could potentially be shifting generations.

Being able to think bigger picture as an entrepreneurial clinician and being able to identify opportunities as they pop up is important.

Separating the clinician, leaving the clinician in the clinical room or the therapeutic space and stepping into owning your role as an entrepreneur or as a director or as a CEO (this has been a big learning journey for me that I'm still evolving in). Give yourself permission to say, 'I'm amazing, the most awesome clinician that I can possibly be and I know I do amazing work.' But to do more or have a bigger reach or whatever your vision is, you need to have the ability to detach, have the awareness.

For me to operate as the best that I can be requires me to have skills in other areas, to be able to keep progressing forward and to ensure that what I'm doing is sustainable.

What opportunities have you seen entrepreneurial thinking offer health professionals and therapists?

1. Addressing our own money issues
That's been the biggest learning for me. I had for a very, very long time and even until very recently, a very difficult relationship with the concept of money.

The driver was never, 'Oh, we can get X amount of sites, which is going to create X amount of revenue.' I didn't even put my rates up in that space for about nine years, because I was just so scared that every time the government contract change that we had to tweak and pivot the way that we provided the program.

I was so scared that if I raised my rates that they wouldn't use us anymore. And if they didn't use us, that meant those clients didn't get the genuine care and support that they needed because they weren't going to be getting it from anywhere else.

But what you realise quickly is that unless you put your rates up and hold your value and you know your value, you can't progress. And if you can't progress you can't sustain and retain with security around what you're already doing.

There are a lot of smart business people with high levels of business acumen out there that have health services and consulting services that charge loads of money, but they don't have the ethics and the values behind it. So I know that what we do comes from the right space and has the right impact.

It's also that responsibility to the people you're taking on the journey. So if I'm going to say to people, 'come on board, share in our vision, come in the direction that we're heading,' if I don't have the capability to have the security behind the business and the structure that we've gotten in place, then I'm at risk of putting those people in an unsafe position in employment. So it's not just about them coming in and having a job with you. It's all the implications in their lives as well. So as an entrepreneur, you're responsible for that.

2. Technology
Technology is evolving, but I'm strong in still wanting that face-to-face connection because I know the power in it, it's at the core of my belief system.

However, generations are shifting. If the only way they're going to reach out to get some help is through a screen as a first step, then we have to meet those needs. Otherwise, we're going to lose the potential to support that generation needing support.

So, I think we need to stretch our brains as clinicians and as entrepreneurs and think we are here, now in five years, where's our industry going to be? We have to try and reverse engineer it because tech isn't going away. We don't even know 10% of what the reality is, of what's already available that we haven't been educated on. Tech services, software systems, social media, everything is evolving. That was definitely not in my remit when I decided to get into this space.

Do you look for agility and willingness to be curious about the future when you hire into your team?

Absolutely. We have a real strong culture of conversation and a culture of invitation, so any thoughts and ideas team members may have are a natural part of our day-to-day engagement. So, we have staff members that have come onboard for one part of the service that we provide and then they'll say, 'Oh, I had an idea about this.' It's like, 'Wow, that's a really cool idea. Let's just map that out a little bit,' and then that thing becomes a reality or something that gets outlined and implemented and that person gets to champion it.

That's not what they were initially enrolled into the

business for. However, that's an area that they had innovation around, and we've been able to help bring it to life and convert it into something tangible they are then championing through the business.

What advice would you like to give to new graduates?

It depends on, again, where the graduates have come from, the type of study they've had and the level of actual hands-on practical engagement and experience. It's all well and good to go and do four years of theory books, it's a very different reality when you're in the room with somebody and they're needing practical, intuitive, logical, connection, care and a partner to go through their journey step by step.

So, if I literally graduated, I'm about to just go into my own thing, I would ask, 'What is the "why" behind that and what does success look like?' I guess a real honest question around this is whether it's the right step now or should there be a bit more exposure first?

You've got to be able to live and breathe what you do.

Chapter five

How you communicate

IF YOU HAVE JUMPED STRAIGHT to this chapter hoping to find the holy grail to effectively market your private practice then you will be disappointed.

You see, marketing, aka communicating your practice to others, can only be done effectively once you know:

1. who you are

2. who you serve.

It really is that simple.

Yet still, I see so many health professionals dashing out to market their practice, looking for the fast, cheap, easy way of bringing in their perfect clients in super quick timeframes. Just because you have credentials does not give you the right to a successful private practice.

You have a responsibility. A responsibility to learn to do this well so you are cared for and so you can be fully present to care for your clients. That is how your practice will remain sustainable for you both.

*Wanting cheap, free and easy marketing
tactics isn't your fault.*

If you're like me, then you've probably spent a lot of money and time trying to implement all the silver bullet marketing techniques that promise thousands of dollars and clients with very minimal work.

This is what I have learned through this process:

1. If I buy a course, but don't do anything with it then nothing changes.

2. If I don't make the time to LEARN what it is I need to be doing, then nothing changes.

3. If I abdicate this learning and pay someone else to do it for me, then I lose my voice, which means my marketing becomes someone else's version of me and I create a message-to-market mismatch so nothing changes.

So forget about all those quick-fix promises.

What I'm about to show you is that we as health professionals have a secret weapon when it comes to communicating who we are.

Your secret glue

Marketing is not a transaction. It's not, 'Hey, read my website, take my business card and book an appointment.' Marketing is about communicating, and communicating is about building rapport and relationships.

As health professionals we are doing this ALL the time. We are actually already experts in this!

Building rapport and relationships is something we do every single day with every single client.

In fact, most of our day when we are working with our clients is spent doing this very thing. This is great news!

Where it gets tricky is understanding that there is a difference between the two and that they follow each other in this sequence:

1. build rapport

2. develop a relationship.

When I run my 'Five Favorite People Networking that Works' training, clinicians of every discipline are always stumped when I ask them what they think rapport is and how if differs from a building a relationship.

We know the textbook answers, rapport is a harmonious working relationship where we feel like we've bonded, but it's also something that is kind of innate so we don't really have to think about it.

The goal of rapport is to get another person thinking, feeling and involved with what you are doing, saying or expressing.

For me, it's when I am:

- paying attention and the other person is paying attention, no one is distracted in the moment

- using common words and phrases with the other person

- feeling like I have known the other for ages and understand their circumstances.

The flip side for the other person is that they feel:

- heard

- safe

- respected.

So we need to communicate with our prospective clients in a way that we are building rapport whether it is:

- face to face – consultations, community events, workshops etc.

- on a phone call – direct inquiries

- online – social media and content marketing (this one is a little bit trickier so we will come back to that later.)

Looking at the three points above, you might feel like you can do the first one or two standing on your head. After all, that is how we traditionally communicate with our clients.

They phone us (or our receptionist), then they come and see us. We spend a great deal of time in that initial consultation to find out more about them, which hopefully leads into another consultation and another…which is when we start to develop a relationship over a period of time.

A period of time is the key here.

Rapport leads into a relationship.

Rapport to a relationship

One we have developed rapport the job isn't done, people are still not ready to 'buy' your services. They are just starting to get to know you, to develop that all-important trust with you.

Clinicians are too quick to assume that initial rapport, no matter how brief or tenuous, will lead to an exchange in value (i.e. a client's money for your expertise). Not true. You still have to put in the hard work to create a long-lasting and fruitful relationship.

To move our clients from rapport to relationship, we have to make it easy for people to engage with us, which involves:

- showing we are interested in THEM

- being ready to answer common questions.

Remember in Chapter 4 when you identified the people you love to serve and their particular problems you are solving? This is where we start to draw on all of that hard work.

You need to give your prospective clients the impression that you know them better than themselves. You do this by using language that they would use, and by asking open-ended questions about where they are at and what they need, which allows them time to think and respond. Then dig and ask more questions so they gradually, over time, begin to open up.

In return, you open up to them about you. This does not mean telling them your life story, but it does mean clearly communicating who you are, who you serve and why.

When you show interest and return that interest, you begin to build rapport and a relationship starts to develop.

Your 5-step communication framework

We communicate differently for different people.

The way you communicate that it's time for your three-year-old to go to bed is different to the way you communicate to your 17-year-old that the garbage needs to be taken out.

The way you communicate with a teenager living with anxiety, trying to navigate a world of online bullying, is going to be very different to the way you communicate with a woman living with anxiety and adjusting to being a first-time mum.

The way you communicate with a young single person will be different to the way you communicate with an elderly couple.

Yet most of the time, we try to reach completely different populations, cohorts or humans with exactly the same messages.

You need to communicate who you are and who you serve with the message that is tailored to the person you are targeting. This is how you start to develop rapport and a relationship with them.

There are five steps you can follow to help you start to communicate more effectively with the right people, no matter if that communication is done face-to-face or online, as shown in Figure 5.1.

YOUR TURN TO MAKE
some magic...

Figure 5.1: The 5-step communication framework

1. **My name is...** Remember, you are a person, not a credential. So you need to humanise and normalise the experience for the people you are relating to.

   My name is Jo. (Yes, it really is that simple.)

2. **I'm an expert in...** I understand that a lot of people feel that 'expert' is a loaded word, however right now

we are not 'treating' or engaging in any therapy, we are trying to meet a prospective client, and when they know we are an expert in something specific then it helps make them feel confident about us.

I'm an expert in helping people return to work following injury, illness and trauma.

3. **I love to help people to...** This is about the problems you love to help people solve.

I love to help people regain a sense of purpose after a period of absence from work. Recovering from injury, illness, or living with a chronic illness and disability is hard. Often people need someone who can help them makes sense of their world and how work fits into their new life, and that's what I do.

4. **I am passionate about...** Share not only your skills and knowledge but also your enthusiasm for your work!

Work is such an important part of our lives and when it's taken away from us, often abruptly, we can feel disillusioned, disempowered and useless. When we can work we have choice, we have purpose, we have identity. Medical science has been telling us for more than 20 years that people who are engaged in work are healthier than those who aren't. That's why I'm passionate about helping people to make their world with work, well – work.

5. **I am best able to help...** Sometimes it's easier to answer this by stating what you don't do. For me that's easy, I don't work with children, I also won't work with perpetrators, and I'm not a good fit for people with addictions. In being able to describe who it is we are best able to help, we are giving potential clients, or people who may want to refer potential clients to us, words to use when describing us.

I am best able to help people who want to work but don't know how to make it work anymore. Sometimes this means helping people return to a job they might need to re-engineer to make it a good fit for them; sometimes this about helping people find a new job. Whatever it is, I am always seeking to make sure that my clients are able to be healthy, learn to manage themselves well and are able to take back control of their lives.

As you can probably see from this example, communicating in the right way to the right people means opening up about yourself and sharing some of your story and why you do what you do.

Now it's your turn to try it out. Use the notes section at the back of the book to help you develop your own personal framework.

This is what helps us to stand out and cut through all the other marketing noise out there.

Without this, then these marketing tools are next to useless:

- social media posts
- FREE things and opt-ins
- FaceBook advertising
- Google adwords
- SEO
- networking events
- offering to speak for FREE.

None of these things will work for you UNLESS you focus on building rapport and a relationship first, which means being willing to mutually exchange value by sharing some of your own personal story.

If you don't know who you are or who your clients are then you won't be communicating effectively in a way they understand you.

Be consistent

This framework works both online and offline. However, you will find navigating the offline world likely easier because, remember, face-to-face is what we traditionally and naturally do in our work.

Learning how to transpose this to an online world is a necessary skill that takes thought, practise and consistency.

The biggest issue I see most people identify when they go through this process is the lack of consistency.

That means consistency in:

- look

- feel

- language

- images

- message.

And consistency across all the platforms you appear.

If you don't have consistency, then you don't have trust.

If you don't have trust, then your potential clients will not buy from you.

If you do not have clients buying from you, then you don't have a business.

You need to show up the same, wherever your clients can find you.

Being consistent matters because I, as a prospective client, want to know that when I read your LinkedIn profile and then go to your website that I have come to the same person and the right place.

I want to know when I've read your About Me Page, and then go your Book A Call page, that it's the same person with the same intention – that intention is to help me.
Your prospective clients are often scared and anxious. They are dealing with all sorts of problems in their life. They do not know you and they do not trust you – yet.

So if you look different and say different things to me in all kinds of different places then I will feel put off. What an inconsistent presence tells me – at often an unconscious level – is this: *I don't belong here I need to find someone else.*

This is obviously a big deal. The last thing you want to do is encourage your potential clients to look elsewhere before you've even had a chance to tell them how much you want to help them!

The TRUE currency of all healthcare is not money, it's not the dollars in our pockets, it's TRUST.

Clients will part with their hard-earned cash when they know they can trust you.

And as we've established earlier, a prospective client who does not trust you will not buy your services. And to be brutally honest, many of our clients are looking for reasons to not come to treatment or therapy. So most of the time we're making it easy for them to NOT to come and get help from us. Now that is not helping anyone is it?

So let go of 'clinician speak' and embrace who you are so that you can talk to those people who you are best able to serve in a way that they can understand you.

Make what you say consistent wherever you say it.

The gift that keeps on giving

When you have a consistent message, you can stop chasing after every new social tactic or hack. Simply ensure that you have a simple, elegant and strategic message that will speak directly to the people you want to serve.

You can turn up to any event and when some asks, 'What do you do?', you can use the consistent message you've developed to confidently state your focus and specialities.

Consistency of the right message helps you know what to do and say – and when to say it – with clarity.

The right message–market fit is a gift. It is a gift that keeps on giving – when we get it right.

It means that your clients, colleagues and peers can recommend you because they know with clarity and confidence what it is you do, who it is you serve, and how you help them.

INTERVIEW
DEAN LAWLER

PHYSIOTHERAPIST
(AKA, PHYSICAL THERAPIST),
CO-DIRECTOR – SPORTS
AND SPINAL PHYSIOTHERAPY CLINICS,
FOUNDER – PRIVATE PRACTICE PREPARED

Dean is a private practice owner of four sites in a regional area of New South Wales, Australia. He has an incredible passion for raising new graduates, and is equally passionate about the communities that he operates in.

You'll find him and his team sharing their knowledge and skills at pretty much any community function. (I've actually had the pleasure of being treated by Dean and one of his team, and I've become migraine-free as a result, something I didn't think was ever going to happen.)

When I first met Dean, he actually asked me for help with his own self-care, which really impressed me. While he has a great business, is living in a beautiful part of the country, he also understands the need to work on himself so that he can continue being a devoted father and husband.

As I got to know Dean further, what excited me was the way he turns his energy and passion into looking after his people. His enthusiasm is what is missing in most other health businesses. Hence, there is much we entrepreneurs can learn from his work.

• •

How did you grow a successful private practice?

Initially, it was trial and error. I'd seen and watched a lot of different practices and the way they treated their staff. It was definitely a path that I didn't want to go down.

I think you need to really value your staff, but also yourself, your own health and your own wellbeing.

There's obviously a lot of other stuff you need to do right, but you need to find your 'why'. Why are you doing what you are doing? If you can grab hold of that, then you set out to make a change and you really want to make a change. That's the path you need to go down.

I get up in the morning, and say, 'I'm going to work today.' And I love that! I genuinely love what I do. I love helping people. Honestly, it was a calling. I knew I was always meant to do that. I genuinely love helping people.

I can fix someone's back pain or neck pain or headaches. That's a drug. I feed off that. That just gives me so much energy. You explain that to young physios, they don't always get it, until they get their first experience with a client that they helped, then they get addicted. It's addictive being a physio and being able to help someone. You've got to truly love what you do first though.

If you're doing it for money, then you're doing it for the wrong reason. Pure and simple.

What does the term entrepreneurial clinician mean to you?

I see opportunities and I know there's opportunities. One of my biggest faults is I've got to stop myself from acting on some opportunities. That's one of my biggest challenges. You talk to my business partner, Rob. He's forever saying to me, 'Dean, you need to keep your brain quiet, seriously. We can't keep doing this, this and this. Stick to one thing at a time, champ.' I find it really hard to. If you count that as being an entrepreneur, being able to see opportunities and have vision then yes, I guess I am, but I don't class myself as an entrepreneur. I think, if you genuinely love what you do, you will reproduce what you do in the best way you can.

If you go into a business thinking, 'I'm going to make X amount of money,' then you're going for the wrong reason. But if you go in the vision of, 'I'm going to help as many people as I can,' then the money will naturally flow from there.

Do a good job, provide a good service, train other people to do what you do. That's the win.

You're incredibly passionate about students and new generations, what do you think they have to offer our thinking and the way we do business?

When I graduated, 20-something plus years ago, I knew I wanted to be a private practice physio. I liked that challenging environment. That's what always drove me. I pretty much came out and I literally faked it until I made it. I didn't know what I was doing, I knew I had the clinical skills to do it, but I didn't have the business skills. I had no idea. No one teaches you business skills at university.

I quickly learnt that there were certain people who I would look up to, from a business point of view. It wasn't always the people I was working with, it was people on the outside. I would look and watch what they did. I thought: that's pretty smart.

So it actually concerns me a little, about the new grads that are coming through because they're not getting an opportunity to go into private practice.

I think the residency statistics in Australia are wild, something like 2300 new grads graduating from physio this year. About 65% of those go out into private practice or want to go into private practice. Yet a lot of the unis are not catering for these new grads to get private practice experience. As a clinic owner that scares the shit out of me.

It terrifies me from a business perspective. There's a lot of time, money and energy spent trying to up-skill a new grad. Why aren't they doing it at university level? When 65% of their graduates go into private practice. It's insane. So, that's one of the things that I'm trying to change. Rob and myself and a couple of physios in Brisbane are trying to change that. We have a Facebook page called Private Practice Prepared. Where we're basically trying to give new grads the skills and tools to be able to survive and thrive in private practice from day one.

That's also why we created a 12-month program, where they don't have to fake it until they make it.

As a result, we've had a lot of clinic owners come to us and go, 'Can we put our new grads through your program?' We do one- or two-day weekend courses. We are in the process of developing an online format where new grads can get some mentoring online. Learn the clinical skills and the business skills that they need be able to go from day one.

You've got to find a good mentor. That's absolutely crucial.

It's not trying to get as many patients in through the door as you can. It's not a sausage factory. It's being able to connect with the patient, engage with them. You engage with them properly and correctly, then they will sell you to their brother, sister, mother.

Engage with the patient and that's how you'll grow.

That's what we're trying to teach, that's what I teach new grads. How to engage with a patient. That's vitally important. I can teach you the good skills of a physio. I can't teach you a personality.

If you can't talk to someone, you can't have a conversation with someone, or be able to ask them what their problem is and be able to listen to that, think about that, turn it over in your head and ask the next appropriate question.

I see there's a massive gap between new grads coming out and what they're taught at university. There is a bit of a push in the physio industry to try and change that. So hopefully that happens.

What do you think the number-one thing is to be successful in a clinical career?

You've got to have vision for what you want. You've got to know what the big and shiny thing is, what the end goal is. That's different for everyone, and that changes over time.

When you have kids, the shiny ball changes and morphs into something different. But you've still got to hold on to a vision of what you want and what you're trying to achieve. Why are you getting up in the morning?

I get up in the morning because I love what I do. My vision has changed a little bit, who I want to help has changed, my values have changed a little bit as well because they change over time when you have a family, or your circumstances change. But you still need to have it.

How do you ensure your own self-care and pay-it-forward to others?

We genuinely love what we do. Rob, my business partner, he's also in the rural fire brigade. So he'll go off and often we'll get a call during trading that he's got to go and put out a bush fire.

To me that's what we do. The patient will understand. We quite often give out fair time to the community. I do a pay-it-forward day, where I'll give you my 25 years of clinical experience and I'll treat you for free. If you genuinely can't afford to come and see a physiotherapist, or an exercise physiologist, please come and see me, I do it every year.

I've actually had the pay-it-forward day extended to other clinics. Someone in Sydney got on my idea and asked me if they could use it, I said, 'Go for it.' It's not my idea, I just had this thought it might be a good thing to do. So please continue on. So, I've had two or three other practices do it since.

I'm trying to get professionals in my area on one day a year to donate clinical skills, whether it be a dentist, psychologist, GP, I don't care. Just donate one day a year to those who are truly in need.

I'm in the position where I can do that. There's a lot of other people in the medical field who could afford to have one day, or half a day. Donate your services to those who really can't afford to access those services.

What future opportunities are there for private practice?

Everyone talks about telehealth, I guess, that is definitely an area for growth. Initially, I still like that hands-on approach first. Then when you get past a certain timeframe I think that you probably could to a telehealth type conference, where it might be reviewing their exercise plans.

We use Physitrack, an online program that has videos and pictures of exercises and is fully interactive. Through Physitrack we can also do a tele conference. So if you're having trouble with those exercises, you click a button and then we can actually look at how you are doing them and correct them via the internet. So that's a pretty good piece of technology.

I've also got a lot of physios or physical therapist friends in the US, and what I'm seeing is a growing concerns of physicians or GPs buying our health practices in the US. They're trying to market their services slightly different to try and capture an audience. That is going to happen here. If you've got your head in the sand about that then you need to pull it out. I think you need to have strategies in place, to try and counteract that in a certain way. One of the ways we're trying to do that is direct access by doing workshops. Again, you're creating a community presence. You're becoming an expert in your field, so to speak.

We've done quite a few headache clinic workshops, where we invite the audience to come in and talk about headaches, and how the headaches can be related to the top three spine processes. Then we invite them in to have an assessment. I think that's an area from a marketing point of view that doesn't get done here in Australia very well. I think there's a growing opportunity for clinicians to market their services down that path.

When GPs start to buy out clinics then it's going to be a bit of a tight squeeze because sometimes that's where your referrals come from. My concern is, I don't want to have the gate keeper control my referrals. I want to control my own referrals. That's all we're trying to do.

People are becoming more and more aware of what they can access, and they're becoming more and more knowledgeable about their own health. Dr. Google is good and bad. It tends to make people a bit more aware of their body, and they tend to ask a lot more questions, that's great. They're asking questions, they're seeking knowledge, but you've got to give them right answers, without fluffing it or sugar-coating it. They'll be thankful for that.

What are the top three things that you would like readers to take away from this interview?

1. It's OK to say no

One thing that I have always struggled with, and I still struggle with it today, and new grads need to learn is it's ok to say no. I still get messages from friends on Facebook at 8:00 at night, or whatever it might be, 'Dean, I've hurt my back, can I see you tomorrow?' I still struggle with saying no. Because that's just my nature, I love to help people. If you can learn to say no, that's for your own personal wellbeing. That way you can look after yourself. It took me a long time to be able to say 'It's okay to say no.' You don't have to fix everyone.

> *You don't have to be the person that fixes everyone.*

2. Find a mentor

You need to have two or three that you follow without Facebook-stalking them. Read their blogs and be interested in what they're saying, what they're presenting. Find three mentors and then you'll end up finding one who you will really resonate with. You need to find one from a clinical point of view, but also from a person point of view. Find someone that you like.

3. Have your vision

Know your 'why', and know what your vision is, why are you doing this? Why are you getting up in the morning? Why do you get up in the morning to do what you do? If it's not because you love what you do, do something else. Because people will see through it if you're faking it. They will know that you've lost interest. If they think for a minute you're just doing this for money they will see right through that, 100%.

And you will lose them forever.

If you truly love what you do, it will come across in your mannerisms, the way you speak to people, the way you carry yourself, how you interact with the other staff members.

WHERE TO NOW?

FIRSTLY, LET'S CELEBRATE THE FACT that who we are is important and what we do is necessary. Hooray!

After all, if we truly want to drive the change that is needed in healthcare then one of the biggest, loudest and most influential players in this system is us: the entrepreneurial clinician.

Without entrepreneurial clinicians in this world, sick people would not get the help they need in a way that they can receive it.

So now that we have just spent a good chunk of time integrating who we are with who we serve and what we do, I can't let this book go without talking about action.
It is time to ask yourself honestly:

What is one thing I can do today to make sure that I put the ideas from this book into action?

I know it's sometimes easier said than done, so here is a very simple framework to help you on your way.

1. **Start small**

   Have a go at one of the exercises in the book and then commit to trying it out for the next 90 days. You can download the worksheets at www.jomuirhead.com/book.

2. **Create accountability**

   Make your intentions visible! I cannot tell you how important it became for me to make the completion for this book very public so that I would stay committed to getting it done. Find a colleague, a peer, a mentor or someone who will help you stay focused on the goals and promises you have made yourself. If you would like to know how I can personally help you go to www.jomuirhead.com/work-with-jo/

3. **Surround yourself with like-minded people**

   Commit to building a tribe of people who know you, get you and have your back. To help you with this, make sure you have subscribed to the Entrepreneurial Clinician podcast that accompanies this book where you can hear all of the interviews recorded live, plus other people interviewed www.jomuirhead.com/podcast.

4. **Stay curious**

   You can't possibly know it all, so let's commit to being curious about our clients, ourselves, our industry and the world we live in. Let go of being a perfectionist, of comparisonitis and fear of missing out (FOMO). I have other resources to support you on this journey www.jomuirhead.com.Above all else, remember the wise words of author Roald Dahl: 'Somewhere inside all of us is the power to change the world.'

5. **Listen to the interviews I conducted for this book.**
There is a series of eight audio tracks available for you to listen to in addition to this book. They are the interviews conducted for this book plus a couple of extras just for you. Take time to listen to them as in the conversation you will find much more gold. You can access them at www.jomuirhead.com/book.

I look forward to seeing and hearing how you go.

Jo

INTERVIEW DETAILS

Angela Lockwood
www.angelalockwood.com.au
Social sites @angelalockwood

Books:

Switch Off: How to Find Calm in a Noisy World (2016), published by John Wiley

The Power of Conscious Choice: How to Make Better Decisions About Things That Matter (2014) published by Bookbound

Mari A Lee
www.thecounselorscoach.com

Books and ebooks

The Gift in the Wound: Stories of Resiliency and Hope (2019)

Healing Betrayal: First Steps for Partners and Spouses of Sex and Pornography Addicts (2018) ebook

The Creative Clinician: Exercises and Activities for Clients and Group Therapy, ebook

Facing Heartbreak: First Steps to Recovery for Partners of Sex Addicts (2012), co author, published by Gentle Path Press

Resources available at www.thecounselorscoach.com

The Complete Therapist Client Forms Packet

The Complete Group Therapy Client Forms Packet

The Employee Policy Manual for Therapists

The Coaching Forms Packet for Coaches

Professional services

Business coaching for therapists and healers –
www.thecounselorscoach.com

The Shine Retreat for Women:
www.shineretreatforwomen.com

Like a Boss – private online group coaching for therapists
and healers: www.thecounselorscoach.com

Growth Counseling Services – counseling services for
individuals located in California, USA:
www.growthcounselingservices.com

Key note and conference presenter, pod cast interview
and media page: www.thecounselorscoach.com

Cathy Love
www.nacre.com.au
Facebook @privatepracticemadeperfect and
@nacreconsulting
LinkedIn @cathylove

Jeffery Jenkins

www.onepointhealth.com.au
Facebook @onepointhealth
LinkedIn @jeffery-jenkins

Anastasia Massouras

www.pureinsights.com.au
www.bringhappyback.com.au
Facebook @anastasiabhb

Dean Lawler

www.physioportmacquarie.com.au
LinkedIn @dean-lawler
Facebook @Private-practice-prepared and
@sportsandspinalportmacquarie

RESOURCES

Books

Beckwith, Harry, 2001, *Selling the Invisible – A Field Guide to Modern Marketing*, Little, Brown & Company, USA

Brockis, Dr Jenny, 2017 *Future Brain: The 12 Keys to Create your High-Performance Brain*, John Wiley and Sons, Australia

Buelow, Beth L, 2015, *The Introvert Entrepreneur*, Ebury Publishing, Great Britain

Cialdini, Robert B, PhD, 2007, *Influence – The Psychology of Persuasion*, Harper Collins, USA

Clason, George S, 1955, *The Richest Man in Babylon*, Penguin Putnam, USA

Drury, John, 2016, *Integrate: Why Work-Life Balance is a Myth and What You Really Need to Create a Fulfilling Lifestyle*, John Drury, Australia

Duckworth, Angela, 2017 *Grit – Why Passion and Resilience are the secrets to success*, Ebury Publishing, Great Britain

Freudenberger, Dr Herbert PhD, 1980, *Burn Out – How to Beat the High Cost of Success*, Bantam Books, USA

Garner, Janine, 2017, *It's Who You Know*, John Wiley and Sons, Australia

Gerber, Michael E, 1995, *The E-Myth Revisited*, Harper Collins, USA

Godin, Seth, 2008, *Tribes: We Need You to Lead Us*, Penguin Putnam, USA

Hammon, Claudia, 2016, *Mind over Money: The Psychology of Money and How to use it Better*, Canongate Books, Great Britain

Hendricks, Gay, 2011, *The Big Leap*, Harper Collins, USA

Loch, Michelle, 2015, *Your Brain is your Business*, Michelle Loch, Australia

Lockwood, Angela, 2017, *Switch Off – How to Find Calm in a Noisy World*, John Wiley and Sons, Australia

Silvoso, Ed, 2002, *Anointed for Business*, Baker Publishing Group, USA

Sinek, Simon, 2009, *Start with Why*, Penguin, Great Britain

Articles and reports

Australian Association of Social Workers, November 2013, 'Tips for Setting Up a Private Practice'

Australian Bureau of Statistics, April 2013, 'Australian Social Trends, Doctors and Nurses'

Royal Australasian College of Physicians, October 2011, Australian and New Zealand consensus statement on the health benefits of work position statement: realising the health benefits of work

Brenton, Jodie, 19 April, 2017, 'The Future of the Psychology Private Practice Industry in Australia', Strive Resource Centre, www.strivecommunity.com.au

Enochs, Elizabeth, February 2015, '11 Things Health Care Professional Wish Everyone Knew', Healthcare Source, www.education.healthcaresource.com

Greenwood, George, 22 September 2017, 'Mental Health Staff on Long Term Sick Leave up 22%', BBC, www.bbc.com/news

Harris, Dehra MD & Glowinski, Anne MD, 31 August 2017, 'The deception at the heart of physician burnout', Kevin MD, www.kevinmd.com

Heller, Robert, 23 November 2005 'The Entrepreneurial Age', Management Issues, www.management-issues.com

Pearl, Robert MD, July 2017, '5 Tips for Breaking Into The Business of Health Care', Forbes, www.forbes.com

Peters, Roger PhD, December 2010, 'Psychology and Private Practice in Australia, Some Inconvenient Truths', Parliament of Australia, www.aph.gov.au

Portoghese et al, revised April 2014, 'Burnout and Workload Among Health Care Workers: The Moderating Role of Job Control', PubMed Central, www.ncbi.nlm.nih.gov/pmc

Power, Clinton, '5 Lessons in How to Create a Profitable Psychotherapy Practice Without Medicare Rebates', Australia Counselling, www.australiacounselling.com.au

World Health Organization, 'Development of a Global Mental Health Action Plan 2013–2020', www.who.int

Websites

NDIS

The National Disability Insurance Scheme (NDIS) provides support to people with disability, their families and carers. The main component of the NDIS is individualised packages of support to eligible people with disability.
www.ndis.gov.au

Physitrack

An online program that has videos and pictures of exercises and is fully interactive to track the progress of patients.
www.physitrack.com

NOTES

NOTES

NOTES